The REAL Girl's KITCHEN

HAYLIE DUFF

razor
bill

AN IMPRINT OF PENGUIN GROUP (USA)

razOr
Bill A division of Penguin Young Readers Group • Published by the Penguin Group • Penguin Group (USA), 345 Hudson Street • New York, New York 10014, U.S.A.

USA / Canada / UK / Ireland / Australia / New Zealand / India / South Africa / China • Penguin Books Ltd, Registered Offices: 80 Strand, London WC2R 0RL, England • For more information about the Penguin Group visit penguin.com • Copyright © 2013 Little Moon Entertainment, Inc. • All rights reserved. No part of this book may be reproduced, scanned, or distributed in any printed or electronic form without permission. Please do not participate in or encourage piracy of copyrighted materials in violation of the author's rights. Purchase only authorized editions. • Published simultaneously in Canada • ISBN: 978-1-59514-683-0 Printed in the United States of America • 1 3 5 7 9 10 8 6 4 2

For my mother. And her mother.

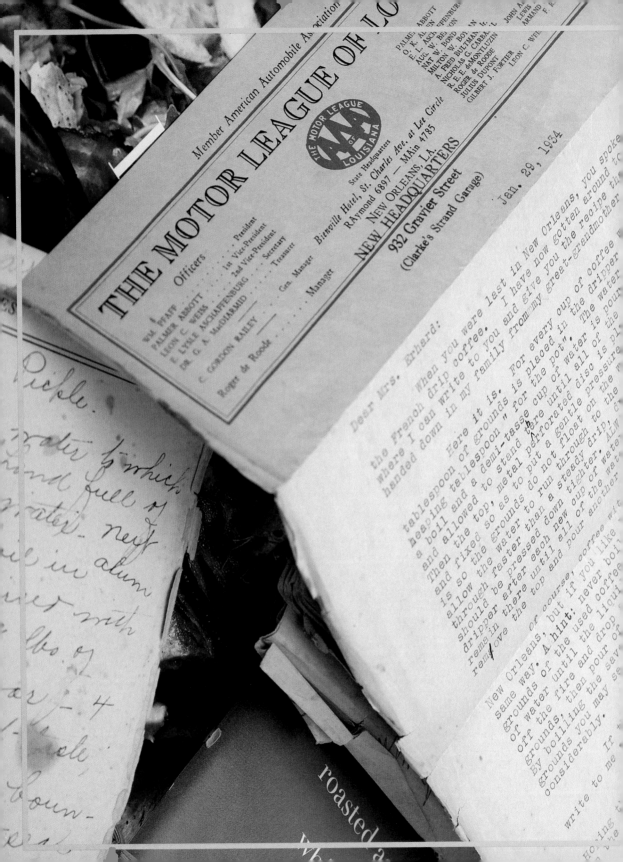

THE MOTOR LEAGUE OF LO[UISIANA]

Member American Automobile Association

Officers

WM. PFAFF .... President
PALMER ABBOTT ...... 1st Vice-President
LEON C. WEISS ...... 2nd Vice-President
E. LYTLE ASCHAFFENBURG .. Secretary
DR. G. A. MacDIARMID ... Treasurer

C. GORDON BAILEY ...... Gen. Manager

Roger de Roode .... Manager

State Headquarters
Bienville Hotel, St. Charles Ave. at Lee Circle
RAymond 6897 — MAin 4785
NEW ORLEANS, LA.
NEW HEADQUARTERS
932 Gravier Street
(Clarke's Strand Garage)

Jan. 29, 1934

Dear Mrs. Erhard:

When you were last in New Orleans, you spoke of
the French drip coffee. I have now gotten around to
where I can write to you and give you the recipe that was
handed down in my family from my great-grandmother

Here it is. For every cup of coffee one
heaping tablespoon of grounds is placed in the dripper
and a demi-tasse cup of water is poured in the water
a boil and allowed to stand there until all of the water
Then the top, metal perforated disc is placed
and fixed so as to put a gentle pressure on the
is so the grounds do not float to the top and
allow the water to run through to the bottom
through be pressed down tighter. Always
should faster than a steady drip. Always
dripper after each new cup of water is poured
remain there until all of the water
remove the top and pour another

New Orleans, but if you like coffee made the
same way. A hint: never boil coffee the
grounds of the used coffee off the fire and drop
of water until the liquid is
grounds, then pour off the water
By boiling the save the grounds you may
considerably.

If
write to me
Hoping

Dear Friends,

For Christmas one year, my dad gave me a real treasure: my great-grandmother's book of family recipes.

It was one of those moments when my past and my present collided in a grand fashion. See, cooking was fairly new to me. For a large portion of my twenties, I spent most of my time focusing on what I SHOULDN'T eat, instead of what I SHOULD eat. But when I made the switch to focusing on eating things that made me happy AND made me feel good, my relationship with food completely changed. I now love to decipher my way through complicated recipes and come up with my own ideas of how to make food taste delicious.

I have come across some real gems in my great-grandmother's book, but my favorite is a simple letter. In 1934, she took a family trip down to New Orleans. Along the way, she met a man named Roger, the owner of a local café. When she returned home, she sent him a letter, politely asking him to share one of his top-secret recipes. He actually sent it to her! He sent his regards and encouraged her to write again.

I would love to think that in this day and age (when our lives are ruled by tweets and text messages) we could still carry on between each other in such a classic way. I love the idea of running out to the mailbox to see if I have received a poignant note from a friend. I love the idea that I could be that friend, sending recipes across state lines simply because they are special. Instead, I would like for this book to give you the same feelings of kindness, warmth, and adventure that my great-grandmother's book gave me.

I'm thankful to have been blessed with a colorful life full of family, food, and laughter. I'm thrilled to be able to share some of my memories with you, and I hope my recipes inspire you to make some great memories of your own.

Love, Haylie

Why Food?

MY FIRST MEMORIES IN THE KITCHEN ARE WITH MY MOTHER AND GRANDMOTHERS. All three of them were good Texas women who loved to cook for the people they love.

My mom's mom is the kind of lady who whipped up impressive feasts of home-made biscuits and gravy, brisket, and jalapeño cornbread. My dad's mom baked. For my fifth birthday she made me a cake shaped like an elaborate carousel, with little ponies at different heights and ribbons of sugary icing. My mom really shines in the chicken and veggie departments but can make you believe in God with one of her cakes.

I love that I grew up in a household that didn't have a "takeout menu drawer," and I was a little ashamed when my mother discovered mine four years ago. She opened the drawer, saw the menus, and gave me this sort of blank stare. It wasn't a look of judgment or anger. She was just wondering where she had gone wrong: how a kid who never knew what Domino's tasted like until she was well into her teenage years had grown up to have a takeout menu drawer.

It sounds small, but that was a real turning point for me. I realized that I was twenty-four and didn't really know how to make anything other than salad. That was it. I was going to learn to cook.

My kitchen attempts as a child involved something I never use now: the microwave. My first order of business? Making a hard-boiled egg. I placed the egg in a small bowl and turned on the timer for six minutes. By minute five that egg had exploded, and there was a thick brown smoke billowing out of the doors of the microwave. Another time, I was preparing a different relic of an earlier life, Easy Mac. I placed the macaroni in a bowl with no water and blasted it for seven minutes. This time the microwave actually caught fire. Bye-bye to microwave number two! Our third microwave met its early demise when I nuked a paper towel over a bowl of marinara sauce and it went up in flames. When I was three microwaves in, my mom took away my "micro privileges."

I was no better on the stove. One time, I caught a mitt on fire as I stirred a soup, and instead of running over to the sink, I stuck my mitted hand into the bubbling pot. Then there was the time I wanted to heat up a can of chicken noodle soup. I turned the burner on and then went to dig out the pot. Before I did this, I set the unopened can directly on top of the electric burner. Being the butterfly chaser I am, I got distracted by something somewhere, and about twelve minutes later that can exploded all over the kitchen. I dropped to the floor because I thought someone had shot at us. My mom and sister died laughing, and I spent the next two hours pulling noodles off the ceiling.

Cooking didn't really click for me until I bought my first home, where I had my own kitchen and a live-in boyfriend whom I wanted to cook for. It's crazy how love changes us. I loved the praise I got from him every time I made us dinner. I got better with each meal I cooked, and pretty soon I had a roster of killer dinners I could whip up in no time. Once I had perfected some dishes, I threw my first dinner party and I was hooked. I loved making my way through the local farmer's markets to shop for unique ingredients. I made fast friends with the owner of a great butcher shop (McCall's in Los Feliz), and even the guys working at the downtown flower marts started to remember me.

I really enjoy the whole experience, from deciding on the menu to the teamwork-style tackling of the dirty dishes at the end of the night. I believe nothing brings people together like a great meal, and I love nothing more than sharing these moments with some of my favorite people.

It still shocks my family members that the girl who blew up numerous microwaves can actually make a pretty mean meal, never mind write her own cookbook. I feel so lucky, and I pinch myself on a regular basis that my one-woman blog has turned into such an incredible gift.

The *Venice* House

A FEW YEARS AGO, I LEARNED TO MEDITATE, AND THE PRACTICE OF STILLNESS HAS BEEN A VERY IMPORTANT PART OF MY LIFE EVER SINCE. It has helped me to find inspiration, sort through mixed emotions, and find clarity during some of my most challenging times. In fact, quite a few of my recipes have been dreamed or discovered during mediation.

During one of my recent mediations I saw myself writing (this book) by the water. I saw myself calm, centered, and inspired. I knew I needed to get to the water, and I needed to do it fast. At the time, I was in the middle of shooting a movie, and I made a deal with myself that as soon as I wrapped, I would head to the beach.

Now, only a few weeks later, I sit at the kitchen window of what we call "the Venice house," which is located in the very artistic and bohemian beach community of the same name. I feel content. I feel like I am exactly where I am meant to be. I have been spending lots of time alone, meeting great new people, trying all kinds of great restaurants, and falling in love with my neighborhood.

On one of the first Sundays I spent in the Venice house, I decided to take a ride to the market and make a healthy dinner. As I rode down Electric Avenue, I noticed that each house had a different fragrance tumbling out of the windows and filling the streets. It was the smell of everyone's dinner. Each one was lovelier than the next. It was the smell of families gathering for a meal. It smelled healthy and delicious. The smells were intoxicating and inspiring. In this moment I realized I was about to go down a very interesting road of self-exploration and discovery. I wasn't just here to write my book. I was here to let go of some things I'd been carrying around like a heavy purse that hadn't been cleaned out in a while. I was here to grow. I was here to move on.

Many of the quantities in this book are listed as "a handful" or "a pinch." Feel free to take little freedoms with amounts of things, like lemon juice. The more intuitive you are, the better the dish will turn out. If you like pine nuts, add them. Extra cherry tomatoes? Add them!

Contents

CHAPTER 1 - BREAKFAST

The Green Smoothie   3
Quinoa, Butternut Squash, Kale, and Fried Egg   4
Ham and Cheese Waffles   9
Mini Egg Pitas   11
Bagel and Lox with Jalapeño Cream Cheese   12

CHAPTER 2 - SALADS

Melon and Burrata with Pesto   18
Herb "Skinny" Salad   21
Haricot Vert Salad   22
Celery, Fennel, and Apple Salad   25
Watermelon Jenga   28
Roasted Beet Salad   33
Horseradish Caesar Salad   34

CHAPTER 3 - SANDWICHES, WRAPS, AND TARTINES

Veggie and Yogurt Sandwich   40
Salmon, Arugula, and Parmesan Wrap   43
Apple and Tuna Salad Sandwich   44
Avocado, Prosciutto, and Radish Tartine   47
Grape, Pecan, and Chicken Salad Sandwich   48

CHAPTER 4 - EGGS ANYTIME

Truffle Deviled Eggs   54
Egg Salad Tartine   57
Kale, Egg, and Ricotta Crostini   58
Fried Egg over Arugula   61
Baked Herb Eggs with Parmesan   62

CHAPTER 5 - I ♥ KALE

"Love" Salad   70
Breadcrumb and Radish Salad   73
Sea Salt and Vinegar Kale Chips   74
Kale, Black Bean, and Butternut Squash Tacos   77
Raw Beet and Kale Salad   78

CHAPTER 6 - SOUPS

Chipotle Tomato Soup   84
Corn Chowder   86
Watermelon Gazpacho   89
Spicy Chicken Noodle "Sick" Soup   90
Shrimp, White Bean, and Kale "Heartbreak" Soup   94

CHAPTER 7 - APPS AND SNACKS

Bacon-Wrapped Dates   98
Sausage and Thyme Stuffed Mushrooms   101
Hummus   102
Mushroom and Herb Crostini   105
Asparagus and Prosciutto Crescent Rolls   106
Burrata and Sun-Dried Tomatoes   111
Baked Buffalo Wings   114

CHAPTER 8 - VEGETABLES

Lime and Cotija Corn   120
Artichoke, Cauliflower, and Pea Gratin   123
Dijon Brussels Sprouts   124
Pecorino and Red Pepper Broccolini   127
Sweet and Spicy Butternut Squash   128

CHAPTER 9 - SUPPER

Simple Grilled Halibut   134
Mussels and Clams over Linguini   137
Lemon Caper Chicken   138
One-Pot Steamed Fish   141
Grape, Goat Cheese, and Rosemary Pizzette   142
Legit Prosciutto-Wrapped Chicken with Shallot Sauce   145

CHAPTER 10 - CHEESE AND CHARCUTERIE PLATES

Cheese Boards   149
Cheese Favorites   151
Maple Bacon   151
Rosemary Marcona Almonds   152
Grilled Asparagus, Mushroom Caps, or Fennel   153
Parmesan Crisps   153
Charcuterie   155

CHAPTER 11 - DESSERTS

Rosemary Olive Oil and Sea Salt over Ice Cream   159
Crescent Roll Apple Pies   160
Strawberry Shortcake in a Mason Jar   163
Nutella Pizza   164
Chocolate-Covered Bacon and Ice Cream   169
Oven S'mores   170

CHAPTER 12 - ESK (EVERYBODY SHOULD KNOW)

Roasted Garlic   175
Simple Grilled Chicken Breast   176
Sun-Dried Tomatoes   179
Roasted Red Peppers   180
Guacamole   183

CHAPTER 13 - DRESSINGS

Real Girl's Kitchen Basic Vinaigrette — 186
Zesty Ranch Dressing — 189
Lemon Tahini Dressing — 190

CHAPTER 14 - TIPS AND TOOLS

Frozen Grapes — 196
Peeling Garlic in a Mason Jar — 196
Olive Oil Hand Moisturizer — 197
Mandolin — 197
Salad Spinner — 197
The Boiling Point — 198
Floss or String for Cutting Cheese — 198
Rose Petals for Decorating Cupcakes — 199

CHAPTER 15 - HERBS

Flat-Leaf Parsley — 207
Sage — 207
Dill — 208
Basil — 208
Cilantro — 209
Rosemary — 209
Herbs de Provence — 210
Mint — 210
Thyme — 211

CHAPTER 16 - DOG TREATS

Bentley's Blend — 214
Baked Dogs Treats — 217

chapter one
BREAKFAST

The Green Smoothie

Quinoa, Butternut Squash, Kale, and Fried Egg

Ham and Cheese Waffles

Mini Egg Pitas

Bagel and Lox with Jalapeño Cream Cheese

My favorite time to enjoy the green smoothie is first thing in the morning. It should be used as a meal replacement.

DURING MY RUN IN THE NORA AND DELIA EPHRON PLAY *LOVE, LOSS, AND WHAT I WORE*, MY FELLOW CAST MEMBER SHARON LAWRENCE GOT ME ADDICTED TO GREEN DRINKS. In addition to being incredibly talented, Sharon has a big heart, lots of energy, *and* stunning skin. I noticed she would sit backstage and sip on these green concoctions before every show, and after a few days, I couldn't help but think those green drinks had something to do with her glow. I had to get the scoop.

Sharon told me she follows an alkaline diet, and the green drinks keep you in the correct pH range. Determined to raise my own pH level, I started researching what I should and shouldn't eat. It seemed pretty easy: lots of greens, veggies, and fruits. No meat, no dairy or processed foods, and lots of lemon. I spent the next few weeks eating that way, and I felt great. My skin was really clear, and any trace of fatigue from performing eight shows a week was gone. Plus, I had lots of energy and a flat belly. I was one happy girl.

After a while, I started to miss meat and bread, and I stopped being so strict with my alkaline diet. But I did walk away with this Sharon-inspired green smoothie! By incorporating the green smoothie into your everyday eating habits, you can still get the health benefits of all these nutrient-rich greens without denying yourself the treats that you crave.

My favorite time to enjoy the green smoothie is first thing in the morning. It should be treated as a meal replacement and is fantastic after a morning workout or hike.

SERVES 1

1 cup filtered or mineral **WATER**
1 handful chopped **ROMAINE**
1 handful **WATERCRESS**
1 handful **BABY SPINACH**
1 handful **FLAT-LEAF PARSLEY**

1 mini **CUCUMBER** (or 1/2 large cucumber)
1 **GREEN APPLE**
1 **BANANA**
Juice of 1/2 **LEMON**

Great additions and substitutes:
mint, agave, lime, ginger, kale, spirulina, ground flax seeds, avocado, jalapeño, pineapple

Use a Vitamix or high-powered blender to blend all ingredients until smooth.

QUINOA, BUTTERNUT SQUASH, KALE, AND *Fried Egg*

THIS BREAKFAST IS HEARTY, DELICIOUS, AND TASTES LIKE FALL. I look forward to the start of the season because I love butternut squash and am always looking for unique ways to incorporate it into my recipes. This breakfast bowl is the perfect solution.

SERVES 1

1 cup uncooked QUINOA (brown rice is a great substitute)
1 BUTTERNUT SQUASH
OLIVE OIL
1 pinch CAYENNE

1 pinch NUTMEG
1 pinch CINNAMON
3 leaves julienned KALE
2 EGGS
SEA SALT and BLACK PEPPER

- -

Soak the quinoa overnight in a small bowl of water.

Preheat the oven to 375 degrees.

Use a vegetable peeler to peel the squash.

Cut the butternut squash in half and scoop out the seeds.

Cut the squash into cubes.

Drizzle with olive oil.

Sprinkle with the cayenne, nutmeg, and cinnamon.

Bake squash for about 40 minutes.

Cook the quinoa according to the package directions.

Massage the kale with a few drops of olive oil.

Fry two eggs in a skillet over medium heat.

Layer everything in a bowl.

Top with sea salt and black pepper.

WAFFLE MIX, prepared according to directions on the package (I like Krusteaz Belgian Waffle Mix)

1 cup CUBED HAM (I like Jennie-O because you can find low-sodium options)

Approx. 1 cup shredded CHEDDAR CHEESE

Generous sprinkling of fresh ground BLACK PEPPER

MAPLE SYRUP

• •

If you read my blog, you know that I can't bake my way out of a paper bag. So, when it comes to making waffle batter, I stick to what is tried and true. I then incorporate all kinds of fun additions to make them feel homemade.

Fold the ham, cheese, and black pepper into the prepared waffle mix.
Coat waffle iron with nonstick spray.
Pour each serving into waffle iron, spreading batter into the corners.
Transfer waffles to plate and drizzle with maple syrup.

Ham and Cheese *Waffles*

THE WEEKEND OF MY SISTER'S WEDDING WAS FILLED WITH ALL KINDS OF FANTASTIC MEMORIES. It was such a special time, with all our family and friends gathered together to celebrate the most important person in the world to me. It felt so surreal that my sister was getting married, but even more surreal that we were OLD enough to get married. I can remember being little girls and dreaming of our big days: where we would have the ceremonies, what our dresses would look like, but more importantly, who would be waiting for us at the end of the aisle.

Hilary chose well. She looked stunning on her wedding day. She wore a blush-colored Vera Wang that fit her perfectly, a high bun on the top of her head, and a glow that no makeup in the world could duplicate. At sunset she turned the corner to walk down the aisle and took everyone's breath away. The ceremony was intimate and the vows were sweet. My mom looked so proud, and I will never forget the way I saw Mike look at Hilary as they lit their unity candles. It really was a perfect moment.

However, the day didn't start that way. We woke up leisurely, without an alarm, and drank coffee together on her patio. I drew her a bubble bath and ordered room service. Ever since we were little we have always had great conversations around a bubble bath, and this morning would be no different. My mom joined us and the three of us sat on the floor of the bathroom, in our bathrobes, eating breakfast. A few minutes later my sister's eyes went wide. She reached into her mouth and pulled out a tooth. I thought she was going to faint. We all started laughing, Hilary included. Then her laughs turned into a cry. I hugged her and reassured her that even if we had to "superglue that thing back in" she was not getting married without her tooth. I've always been the big sister and even though she is all grown up, it made me feel good to know that hasn't changed.

Thankfully, Hilary's wedding planner swooped in and saved the day. She had my sister in a dentist's chair and back to the hotel in forty minutes. They say it's good luck if it rains on your wedding day. I think the same can be said about losing a tooth.

3 MINI PITAS
2–3 EGGS
1 tablespoon MILK
1–2 tablespoons shredded HAVARTI

1 tablespoon chopped CHIVES
A few CHERRY TOMATOES
1 cup SPINACH

Make a 2–3 inch slice in the sides of the pitas.
Toast pitas until slightly browned.
Crack 2–3 eggs in a small mixing bowl.
Add the tablespoon of milk.
Whisk until blended.
Pour eggs in a skillet over medium-low heat.
Add havarti, chives, tomatoes, and spinach.
Fold the eggs as you scramble them.
Arrange eggs in pitas.

SOME MORNINGS I HIT SNOOZE ONE TOO MANY TIMES AND MY USUAL MORNING BREAKFAST ROUTINE GETS THROWN INTO FAST-FORWARD. This recipe is perfect for the girl on the go. By slow cooking the scrambled eggs you will even have enough time to throw on a bit of makeup as your breakfast cooks. I promise you will be happy you ate something homemade instead of grabbing the chocolate muffin that always taunts you at your local coffee shop. So make these pitas, grab a napkin, and hit the road.

Bagel AND *Lox* WITH JALAPEÑO CREAM CHEESE

THIS BREAKFAST ALWAYS REMINDS ME OF MY BROTHER-IN-LAW, MIKE. Without fail, he orders lox and a toasted bagel *every* time we have breakfast together. I first took notice of his obsession while we were all on vacation together in Hawaii. Every morning my sister, Hilary, and I would be so excited to get up early and explore the buffet. It was filled with made-to-order omelets, beautiful fresh fruits, and even a fabulous miso soup. Our plates ended up looking like a sampler platter with one or two bites of each item it offered. It was our version of heaven.

But Mike's breakfast was a different story. It was always simple: a toasted bagel, some fresh lox, a good spread of cream cheese, and a couple of capers. We were there for five days, and he ordered the same thing every single day. I like his style though, and I think it really speaks to his character. I find something very comforting about a man that knows what he likes and sticks with it. Years later, Mike is still ordering a bagel with lox every chance he gets.

The day after my nephew, Luca, was born, Mike and I walked across the street from Cedars-Sinai to Jerry's Famous Deli and picked up bagels with lox for all of us. I couldn't help but feel like life had really come full circle. The first time I remember eating a bagel and lox with Mike, he and Hilary had just met. The next time that I really took notice of it, they had just married. Now, here we sat with our bagels and lox and their new bundle of joy. I wonder if Luca will grow up liking the same breakfast as his dad. I can't wait to find out, and I can't wait to enjoy it with him.

SERVES 4

8 ounces **WHIPPED CREAM CHEESE**	4 ounces **LOX**
1 sliced **JALAPEÑO**	1 sliced **TOMATO**
4 **BAGELS**	**CAPERS** or **CAPER BERRIES**

Use a food processor to blend a few jalapeño rings into the cream cheese.

Toast bagels.

Spread cream cheese on bagels.

Layer on lox, tomato, and capers.

NOTE: Purple onion, sprouts, and cucumbers are a great addition to this platter.

13

chapter two
SALADS

Melon and Burrata with Pesto

Herb "Skinny" Salad

Haricot Vert Salad

Celery, Fennel, and Apple Salad

Watermelon Jenga

Roasted Beet Salad

Horseradish Caesar Salad

Melon and Burrata with Pesto

WHEN I WAS COMPILING THE RECIPES THAT I FELT SHOULD BE INCLUDED IN THIS BOOK, I KNEW I HAD TO INCLUDE SOME VARIATION ON A CAPRESE SALAD. It is, after all, one of my favorite dishes. I love to eat it poolside on vacation, as a starter when I'm out to dinner, or as a snack when I'm lounging around the house.

So, without straying too far from a classic dish that I love, I give you this one. I like to think of it as my version of a caprese salad (even though I know that technically it isn't). The melon gives a great burst of sweetness, the burrata treats us to its eternal creaminess, and the zesty pesto brings life to every bite. Try this at your next dinner party—and don't forget to check your teeth!

SERVES 4

1 MELON
1 handful BURRATA
2 cups FRESH BASIL
3 cloves GARLIC
1 tablespoon OLIVE OIL
1/3 cup PINE NUTS

1 teaspoon LEMON JUICE
1 pinch LEMON ZEST
1/2 teaspoon CRUSHED RED PEPPER
1/2 teaspoon SEA SALT
1/2 teaspoon BLACK PEPPER

Remove seeds and rinds from melon.
Slice melon into thin pieces.
Arrange the sliced melon on a plate in a fan.
Roll a handful of burrata into a ball.
Place the burrata in the center of the plate.

PESTO
Combine basil, garlic, olive oil, pine nuts, lemon juice and zest, red pepper, sea salt, and black pepper in a Vitamix or food processor.
Blend until desired thickness (I like mine on the thicker side).
Place a scoop of the pesto on top of the burrata.
Let the pesto slide over the cheese.

KEEP IN MIND THAT JUST BECAUSE YOU ARE EATING SALAD DOESN'T MEAN YOU ARE CUTTING CALORIES. YUMMY DRESSINGS CAN BE A CALORIC NIGHTMARE. THE BEAUTY OF THIS SALAD IS THAT IT'S ALMOST DRESSING-FREE. THE OLIVE OIL, LEMON, AND HERBS PACK SUCH A MAJOR FLAVOR PUNCH, YOU WON'T EVEN MISS IT. SO PILE ON THE VEGGIES AND CHOW DOWN—GUILT-FREE.

HERB "*Skinny*" SALAD

THIS SALAD CAME TO ME DURING A MAJOR DIET PHASE IN MY LIFE. I had just wrapped a movie that filmed in Baton Rouge, where I had been living on gumbo, alligator po'boys (one of my favorites), and jalapeño hush puppies. Every weekend my rental car and I would venture down to New Orleans for a change of scenery and some serious soul food. I loved spending my evenings dining among all the beautiful old buildings and listening to the music from a broken-in saxophone fill the streets while I ate my weight in crawfish.

The people and the food of the South make me happy down to the deepest part of my heart, but after all that food and fun, it's fair to say I came home a few pounds heavier than when I left. It was definitely time for me to clean up my diet and load up on some greens.

SERVES 1-2

3 cups MIXED BABY GREENS
LETTUCE
1 handful halved CHERRY TOMATOES
1/4 cup TOASTED PINE NUTS
1/2 cup chopped FLAT-LEAF PARSLEY
1/2 cup chopped MINT
1/2 cup chopped DILL
1/4 cup chopped CHIVES

1 thinly sliced CARROT
5 thinly sliced RADISHES
1/2 cup thinly sliced CUCUMBER
1 cubed AVOCADO
OLIVE OIL
Juice of 1 LEMON
1 teaspoon COARSE SEA SALT

Wash and dry mixed greens.
Toss all ingredients in a large mixing bowl with the olive oil, lemon juice, and sea salt.

Extra benefits:
• Flat-leaf parsley is a natural diuretic.
• Radishes are an ultimate superfood. They fill you up quickly, freshen your breath, and even aid in banishing headaches. Load up your "Skinny" salad with lots of these.
• Pine nuts are a great source of protein, and these tiny little nuts also banish hunger pangs.

Haricot Vert SALAD

MY GRANDMOTHER, NANNY, WAS AN OLD FASHIONED, GOOD-HEARTED SOUTHERN WOMAN. She doled out the best hugs, loved to brush my hair, lived for *Murder She Wrote*, and would make no apologies after she beat your ass at a good hand of gin rummy. I loved to stay with her for the weekend, and my sister and I used to spend hours snooping through her bathroom and her jewelry box. Trying on her big bras and extensive collection of muumuus provided us with hours of entertainment.

My favorite anecdote about Nanny is that she used to hide her jewelry in the washing machine when she went out of town, claiming that "burglars would never look in there."

I always loved cooking with Nanny; there was no such thing as a calorie and never enough salt! I also learned a lot of skills from her, including how to snap green beans. When I was five years old, she sat me up in the center of her kitchen table and gave me a big bag of string beans with two bowls: one for the ends, the other for the snapped parts. We would laugh and snap until the tips of my fingers felt numb. She had the absolute best laugh—the kind you could pick out of a crowd—but still managed to be ladylike. Sometimes I can still hear her laughter, and I can't cook a green bean without thinking of her.

SERVES 2

2 handfuls HARICOT VERTS
1 handful CHERRY TOMATOES
1 handful chopped DILL

1 teaspoon WHOLE-GRAIN MUSTARD
1 splash RED WINE VINEGAR
1 pinch SEA SALT

Boil beans in a big pot for about 6 minutes.
Remove beans from heat.
Drain the beans and place them in a bowl of cold water.
Let cool.
Add cherry tomatoes, dill, mustard, vinegar, and salt.
Toss and enjoy.

1 GREEN APPLE
2 CELERY STALKS
1 FENNEL BULB
2 tablespoons PARMESAN
1 tablespoon chopped DILL

1 tablespoon chopped THYME
Juice of 1 LEMON
Drizzle of OLIVE OIL
SEA SALT and BLACK PEPPER
to taste

• •

Thinly slice the apple, celery, and fennel.
Toss with the parmesan and herbs.
Drizzle with lemon juice and olive oil.
Add a pinch of sea salt and black pepper.

Celery, Fennel, AND Apple SALAD

I HAD JUST SPENT THE MAJORITY OF THE SUMMER WORKING ON A MOVIE IN THE MIDDLE OF NOWHERE. For two months, we were working long hours, covered in dirt and fake blood. I needed to blow off some steam and had all kinds of rowdy energy running through my veins. I had been seeing this guy for a few months, but the movie had taken up every minute of my time. The night that I wrapped, he asked to take me out for a celebratory dinner, and I was in serious need of some romance.

We went to one of our favorite sushi restaurants, and after dinner we weren't ready to go home yet. We walked down the street to a dark little restaurant that has a fantastic patio bar. We snuck past the line of waiting customers with reservations and sneakily snagged a table before the hostess knew it was available. We ordered a nice bottle of wine and an apple salad to share. I remember him teasing me for ordering a plate of apples, but neither one of us was complaining once it arrived.

Normally, we hated those couples that sit on the same side of the booth with each other, but that night we chose to ignore our usual rule. (I ignored a lot of my usual rules with this guy.) After we were onto our second bottle of wine, I excused myself to go to the restroom. What happened next will go down as one of my favorite make-out sessions in all of my kissing history.

I opened the door to the restroom and found him waiting there. He quietly pushed me back into the stall and shut the door as he pulled me into a kiss. It felt like we sank into each other. It was scandalous, frisky, and fun. A minute or two later we both walked past the line of people waiting for the restroom and back to our table as if nothing had happened. We finished the apple salad and the second bottle of wine and poured ourselves into a cab. It was the perfect way to end a long shoot and a great way to spend a Friday night. He is still a dear friend of mine. We have managed to sneak in a few good kisses over the years but never one quite as memorable as that one.

Watermelon JENGA

MY FRIEND BEVERLEY AND I MET WHILE I WAS WORKING ON 7TH HEAVEN, WHERE I WAS THE NEW KID ON THE BLOCK AND SHE HAD BEEN IN EVERY EPISODE FOR THE LAST EIGHT YEARS. I was so excited to be on the show that I would wake up extra early every day to put on a cute outfit before work. I would walk into the hair-and-makeup trailer in a pair of platforms at five A.M., and Bev's eyes would roll into the back of her head. She thought I looked totally ridiculous, and I did. Finally, I asked her why we weren't hanging out, and she broke it down for me.

She said, "You come into work all dressed up everyday. Don't you own a pair of sweatpants?"

I thought to myself, *That's it? A pair of sweatpants is the only thing standing in the way of this friendship?*

The next day I rolled into work in a big, baggy pair of sweats, with no makeup and my hair in a messy bun on the top of my head. I looked like I had just crawled out of bed. I glanced over, and Bev was grinning from ear to ear. Her exact words to me were, "Haylie, there you are. Nice to meet you," and we have been the closest of friends ever since. I will be forever grateful for those sweatpants; because of them I have a lifelong friend. Bev gives the greatest advice, and I was the first in line to visit after she welcomed her daughter into the world.

Bev was sitting on my kitchen counter when I thought up this appetizer. We were hungry, and the only things in my refrigerator were watermelon, tofu, feta cheese, eggs, olives, and some old tortillas. Then, as I was looking at these cubes of watermelon, it hit me. As we talked, I started building. I grabbed some mint from my yard and drizzled some olive oil and balsamic vinegar across the top.

One bite and we were in love. In that moment, we were just two old friends sitting on the kitchen counter together like kids, building a tower out of watermelon.

1 **SEEDLESS** WATERMELON
1 8-ounce block FETA
A few MINT LEAVES

OLIVE OIL to garnish
BALSAMIC VINEGAR to garnish
SEA SALT

Cut watermelon and feta into cubes of matching size.

Build the tower.

Sprinkle the mint.

Drizzle the oil and vinegar.

Sprinkle with a pinch of salt.

4 ROASTED BEETS
3 cups BUTTER LETTUCE
1/4 cup CRACKED HAZELNUTS
1–2 tablespoons GOAT CHEESE
1 tablespoon OLIVE OIL

1 tablespoon HAZELNUT OIL
1 teaspoon SHERRY VINEGAR
½ teaspoon HONEY
SEA SALT and BLACK PEPPER

Roasted Beets

Roasted beets are available at many grocery stores, usually in a package of 4, but you can also roast them yourself.

Scrub beets well and remove greens.

Bake at 400 degrees for 50–60 minutes, checking them every 20 minutes until tender.

Layer butter lettuce over the plate.

Slice the beets and pile onto the greens.

Add hazelnuts and goat cheese.

Drizzle with dressing.

Dressing

Combine olive oil, hazelnut oil, sherry vinegar, honey, sea salt, and black pepper in a mason jar and shake to emulsify.

Roasted Beet SALAD

THIS SALAD ALWAYS REMINDS ME OF ONE OF MY FAVORITE GIRL-FRIENDS, EMMANUELLE. She is intelligent, fun, and drop-dead gorgeous. She is open and present but just aloof enough to be wildly mysterious. Anytime one of my guy friends meets her, he is instantly left swooning. The night I broke up with my last serious boyfriend, the only place I wanted to be was sitting at a dinner table across from her, because I knew she would make me laugh and have some bright outlook about my newly single status.

Em and I weren't always soul sisters. I used to date one of her close guy friends, who wasn't very fond of me by the end of our relationship. Being the loyal friend that she is, Em wasn't very fond of me either.

The first time we hung out was during our friend Jenna's wedding, where we were both bridesmaids. She was Jenna's longtime best friend (and maid of honor) and I was the new best friend. Both wanting to be her favorite, we bumped heads a bit. Over the following year, we became more cordial and found ourselves actually enjoying each other's company. We still needed that one moment when you find yourself on the same wavelength. Then, on New Year's Eve, it happened.

We were sitting at one of the big fancy steakhouses in Las Vegas, at a table of about twenty people. In an attempt to make us get along, Jenna sat us next to each other. Drinks arrived, we placed our orders, and our common ground quickly presented itself.

"May I have the grilled whitefish, sauce on the side, and instead of potatoes may I please have the sautéed greens and a side order of grilled asparagus?" we both said.

Neither of us heard what the other one ordered, but when the food arrived we couldn't help but laugh. Everyone else had ordered steaks or roasted chicken, and we had matching whitefish plates, with the same substitutions and everything. I had met my food twin. Em looked at me with her big brown eyes and said, "When we get back to LA, can we please go have dinner? We are meant to be friends, I just know it."

A couple of weeks later, we were sitting on the patio at Il Sole eating yet another matching dinner (their famous beet salad). I love that no matter where we are eating or how far away from me she is sitting at the table, we always end up ordering the same thing. Our food-twin wavelength has now carried over through many other aspects of our lives. No matter how busy we are or where in the world we happen to be, we always seem to know the right time to call. It makes me feel good to know that sometimes all you need is a tiny piece of common ground to find exactly whom you need in your life.

Horseradish Caesar SALAD

WHEN I STARTED TO WRITE THIS BOOK, MY BABY SISTER, HILARY, WAS NINE MONTHS PREGNANT. Thankfully she had an easy pregnancy without any complications, but of course with pregnancy comes all kinds of interesting food choices, and I was all too happy to go down that road with her.

For the first two months of her pregnancy, she craved Red Hots candy, which she snacked on constantly. After the Red Hots came the grilled octopus. Girlfriend and I have eaten enough grilled octopus to feed a small country. Everywhere we went she asked for it, and when we found a place that served it, her big bright eyes would light up like the Christmas tree at the Grove. Then came the truffles. We are both self-proclaimed truffle pigs, and once that craving kicked in, I was thrilled to go out for as many dinners as she wanted. One night, we made crostini with bubbly blue cheese, prosciutto with its edges barely crispy from the oven, and truffle honey spilling over the top. Seriously, if I could only eat one thing forever, it might be that.

When my sister was two days past her due date, she tried every trick in the book to induce labor: shots of balsamic vinegar and even a special "pregnancy salad" that claimed it would help. Nothing worked. So to take her mind off things, we decided to go out for our favorite salad, a spicy Caesar. Hil had heard that spicy foods and horseradish help to move things along, so just like a good sister does, I obliged, and we shared the Caesar. Extra spicy.

When I tell you that this salad lit us on fire, I am not exaggerating. It burned right to the deepest parts of our noses and made our eyes swell with big, salty tears. This was unlike any pain I have ever experienced. With our sweaty foreheads, burning noses, and tears running down our faces, we looked up at each other and just laughed. And then our laughter took a beautiful shift. With two hands on her belly, one hers and one mine, we both realized the lengths we were already willing to go for this kid. In that moment I realized how proud I am of my sister and how much we already loved the little guy that was about to change all of our lives forever.

I love this version of Caesar salad dressing because it's significantly healthier than the usual version made of mayonnaise and eggs. The yogurt provides the creamy texture here, and you cut out the fat. If you like it spicy, just add extra horseradish, and if you want to thin it out, add filtered water.

1 cup fat-free GREEK YOGURT
1 tablespoon DIJON MUSTARD
Juice of 1 LEMON
1 small pinch SEA SALT and
BLACK PEPPER
1 tablespoon HORSERADISH

2 pressed cloves GARLIC
1 splash WORCESTERSHIRE
6–8 splashes TABASCO
3 cups washed and chopped ROMAINE
LETTUCE
Grated PARMESAN

Mix all ingredients except the romaine and parmesan into a dressing in a small bowl.

Drizzle mixture across the lettuce.

Garnish with grated parmesan.

Serve on a chilled plate.

chapter three
SANDWICHES, WRAPS, AND TARTINES

Veggie and Yogurt Sandwich

Salmon, Arugula, and Parmesan Wrap

Apple and Tuna Salad Sandwich

Avocado, Prosciutto, and Radish Tartine

Grape, Pecan, and Chicken Salad Sandwich

Veggie and Yogurt SANDWICH

I FIRST DISCOVERED THIS SANDWICH WHILE I WAS ON LOCATION IN TORONTO. On my days off, I loved to wander around Yorkeville, and I eventually found my way to Pusateri's, a gourmet food shop filled with everything you could ever dream of snacking on. Toronto was freezing cold, and snow was piled knee-high in every direction, so finding a pretty green avocado was a treat. It was love at first bite with this sandwich, and when you make it, you will immediately understand what I'm talking about. The cucumbers and carrots provide a thirst-quenching crunchy texture, the avocado and yogurt make it smooth, and the walnuts seem to bring it all together. It's a fantastic combination and is great in a wrap too!

SERVES 1

1 cup fat-free GREEK YOGURT
2 sprigs chopped fresh DILL
2 sprigs chopped fresh MINT
2 slices OAT BREAD
1 pinch SEA SALT

1 sliced CARROT
1 sliced AVOCADO
6-8 slices CUCUMBER
1 handful ARUGULA SPROUTS
1 handful CHOPPED WALNUTS

Mix yogurt, dill, and mint in a small mixing bowl.
Spread across both sides of bread.
Sprinkle with sea salt.
Layer remaining ingredients.
Enjoy.

Wild-Caught Salmon versus Farmed Salmon

Here's the deal . . . I will almost always encourage you to buy cage-free, organic, low sodium, blah, blah, blah. It doesn't always really matter if you do or you don't. I understand that organic produce is sometimes more expensive. The farmer's market can be a great solution! However, in the case of wild-caught versus farmed fish you MUST choose the wild-caught. More often than not, the farms are unsanitary and the pens are overcrowded. The fish are fed dyes and antibiotics, and if they are eating it, so are you. So let's support the fishermen, not the fish farms.

Salmon, Arugula, and Parmesan Wrap

THESE LIGHT AND REFRESHING WRAPS ARE A GREAT SUMMERTIME MEAL. In fact, this was our go-to meal one summer. My sister and I asked my mom to make us these wraps almost every day. Being the sweet mom that she is, she stocked up on the ingredients and happily made them for us. I'm sure she was happy when our salmon wrap addiction ended. I love that you can make these ahead of time, and the easy assembly makes them perfect for a pool party.

SERVES 1

1 steak WILD-CAUGHT SALMON
2 tablespoons LIGHT CREAM CHEESE
LAVASH WRAP or TORTILLA

2 cups ARUGULA
1 tablespoon OLIVE OIL
1 LEMON WEDGE
2 tablespoons grated PARMESAN

Grill the salmon on medium heat. Remove from heat and let cool.

Spread a thin layer of cream cheese across the lavash wrap or tortilla.

Arrange salmon and arugula on the wrap.

Drizzle with olive oil and a squeeze of lemon.

Sprinkle with grated parmesan.

Roll it up.

NOTE: To save time, you can also buy wild-caught salmon in a can.

Apple AND *Tuna Salad* SANDWICH

MUCH LIKE EGG SALAD, I DON'T USUALLY MEET A TUNA SALAD I LIKE. I wish I was one of those people who can skip the mayonnaise and still enjoy it . . . but I'm not. What I do enjoy is the crunch of pickles, the sweetness of apples, and the nutty flavor of walnuts. This isn't the cafeteria-style tuna salad you probably hated as a kid. In fact, kids will actually want to eat this one!

SERVES 1

1 package LIGHT TUNA IN WATER
2 tablespoons LIGHT MAYONNAISE
1 tablespoon DIJON MUSTARD
2 chopped DILL PICKLES
1 handful CHOPPED WALNUTS
1 cored and chopped GREEN
APPLE (skin optional)

SEA SALT
LEMON PEPPER
1 cup BUTTER LETTUCE
GRAINY SANDWICH BREAD

Combine all ingredients except lettuce and bread in a mixing bowl.
Toast bread.
Layer butter lettuce and tuna salad on bread.

Avocado, Prosciutto, AND *Radish* TARTINE

A WEEK OR SO AFTER I MOVED TO THE VENICE HOUSE, MY MOM CAME TO SPEND A WEEKEND WITH ME. She was so relaxed and happy, and it was nice to spend some quality time with her, taking walks, going on bike rides, and sitting in the backyard with the dogs.

One morning we woke up early and decided to go watch the cute early morning surfers at the beach. We rode our bikes to Gjelina Take Away, got two cortados to go, and two avocado and radish tartines. We made our way to the beach and found a perfect spot to sit and watch the surfers catch waves as the sun came up. The air was cool and crisp, our coffees were warm, and sharing this moment with my mom made my heart warm too.

SERVES 2

4 slices FRENCH BREAD
2 AVOCADOS
1 LEMON WEDGE

2 thinly sliced RADISHES
4 slices PROSCIUTTO
SEA SALT

Preheat the oven to 350 degrees.
Bake the sliced bread for 10 minutes or until browned.
Remove and let cool.
In a small mixing bowl, lightly mash the avocados.
Add a small squeeze of lemon.
Layer prosciutto, avocado, and radish on the bread.
Sprinkle with sea salt.

Grape, Pecan, AND Chicken Salad SANDWICH

CHICKEN SANDWICHES ALWAYS REMIND ME OF THE AFTER-SCHOOL SNACKS THAT MY MOM WOULD MAKE US WHEN WE WERE KIDS. We lived in the hill country for a couple of years, and we drove forty-five minutes to school and back everyday. During the warmer months, my mom would take us to the New Braunfels River instead of heading straight home. We would eat a snack and hurry to finish our homework, just dying to hop on our black rubber tubes and hit the crystal-clear water. We would catch crayfish and play with little frogs until the sun went down. On the ride home my mom would hand us a sandwich in a Ziploc bag, usually wrapped with a napkin. Her chicken salad sandwich has always been my favorite. Here is my best attempt at re-creating her classic.

SERVES 1

1 boiled and chopped CHICKEN BREAST
1 tablespoon MAYONNAISE
1 tablespoon DIJON MUSTARD
1 handful CRUSHED PECANS
1 handful halved PURPLE GRAPES

2 stalks finely chopped CELERY
2 sprigs chopped TARRAGON
PEA SHOOTS (optional)
BREAD

Mix all ingredients except bread in a mixing bowl.
Toast bread.
Layer mixture onto toasted bread.

chapter four
EGGS ANYTIME

Truffle Deviled Eggs

Egg Salad Tartine

Kale, Egg, and Ricotta Crostini

Fried Egg over Arugula

Baked Herb Eggs with Parmesan

Truffle *Deviled Eggs*

IN MY FAMILY, WE LOVE TO TELL THE SAME STORIES OVER AND OVER AGAIN. Our deviled eggs story is one of our favorites. When we tell this story, we can't help but laugh. It reminds us of a time when we had these big Hollywood dreams and life seemed really simple.

My mom, Hilary, and I had just moved to Los Angeles, and our one-bedroom apartment was more than a little bare. Across the courtyard from us was an empty two-bedroom apartment that the complex used as a storage unit. One afternoon as my mom was making deviled eggs, Hilary and I decided to go on a little adventure. We hopped over the balcony of the storage apartment and slipped in through the sliding door. There were couches piled on top of each other, tables stacked to the ceiling, and lamps pushed into any available space. We made a few trips back and forth, slowly furnishing our unfurnished apartment with our new "borrowed" treasures.

During our final trip to the storage apartment we heard noises coming from the front door. We hid among the clutter and quickly realized that the employees used this apartment for their lunch break. Hilary and I were stuck! We could see my mom sitting on our balcony, peeling hard-boiled eggs and laughing at us. We spent the next thirty minutes trying to conceal our giggles while the guys ate their lunch. Once they finally finished, we ran back to our apartment with a coffee table balanced across our shoulders. When we finally made it out of that apartment, we were sure to leave all of our borrowed furniture behind.

Now, with our busy schedules and grown-up lives, we look back at our years spent at the Oakwood apartments and can't help but smile. We had no idea the roller coaster that life was about to take us on, and we have been so blessed. Hilary is still my favorite person to get into mischief with. Last year we had the phrase "Thick as Thieves" scrawled down the inside of our forearms. I don't think we intended for our tattoos to symbolize the time that we actually *were* thieves, but I can't help but see the irony.

12 EGGS
2 tablespoons MAYONNAISE
1 tablespoon TRUFFLE OIL

1 teaspoon TRUFFLE SALT
Grated FRESH TRUFFLE (if available)
FROSTING BAG or FREEZER BAG

Place eggs in a pot of cold water.

Bring water to a boil.

Turn off heat and let eggs sit in the hot water for 7 minutes.

Remove from water.

Let eggs cool in a bowl of fresh cold water.

Peel off the shells.

Slice eggs in half and set aside the yolks in a separate mixing bowl.

Add mayonnaise, truffle oil, and truffle salt.

Mix until smooth and creamy.

Adjust ingredients to taste.

Spoon mixture into the bag.

Cut the corner of bag.

Fill each egg white with the truffle-yolk mixture.

Die of happiness.

WHOLE FOODS, TRADER JOE'S, AND MANY OTHER GROCERY STORES SELL PEELED HARD-BOILED EGGS. NO BOILING, AND NO TIME SPENT PEELING THE EGGS. YOU CAN SKIP ALL THE FRUSTRATION. YOU'RE WELCOME.

Egg Salad TARTINE

WHEN I WAS GROWING UP, I THOUGHT EGG SALAD WAS SO GROSS. My grandma loved it, but to me it always looked mushy and funky. The few times I actually tried it, I bit into big chunks of raw onion and felt overpowered by the mayonnaise. Determined to find a version I enjoyed, I started experimenting.

I wanted to stay true to the shape of the eggs instead of mashing them into a bowl of mush. I wanted to skip the raw onion altogether and avoid using mayonnaise. After some trial and error, I finally created an egg salad that I crave on a regular basis. Nanny would be so proud.

YIELD: ABOUT 4 HALF-CUP SERVINGS

5–6 HARD-BOILED EGGS
1 stalk thinly sliced CELERY
6 stems chopped CHIVES
1 tablespoon fat-free GREEK YOGURT
Tiny squeeze LEMON JUICE
1 teaspoon CAPERS

1 pinch PAPRIKA
1 pinch SEA SALT and BLACK PEPPER
CROSTINI (sliced and toasted sourdough or French baguette)
Chopped DILL to garnish

Slice the eggs into rings and set aside half.
Mash the other half gently with a fork.
Combine the eggs in a mixing bowl.
Add remaining ingredients.
Try to avoid over-mashing the eggs.
Arrange on the crostini and garnish with the chopped dill.

KALE, *Egg,* AND RICOTTA *Crostini*

I AM MOST OFTEN INSPIRED BY THE FOOD THAT I GREW UP EATING AS A CHILD, BUT THIS RECIPE IS ONE INSPIRED BY MY LIFE IN LA. Leave it to LA people to eat greens with their eggs! It sounds like a bizarre combination, but this is my go-to breakfast on most occasions, and it makes a killer late-night snack. These crostini are a more amped-up version of my usual fried egg and arugula and a great dish to serve for brunch.

SERVES 4

4 slices BAGUETTE, or the bread of your choice
4 EGGS
1/4 cup GOAT CHEESE
1/4 cup RICOTTA

Juice of 1/2 LEMON
6–7 stems chopped CHIVES
OLIVE OIL
4 leaves TUSCAN KALE
1 pinch SEA SALT and BLACK PEPPER

Preheat the oven to 350 degrees.
Bake the bread slices and remove when toasty brown.
Set aside and let cool.
Fry the egg on medium heat in a frying pan (avoid cooking or breaking the yolk).
Mix goat cheese, ricotta, lemon juice, and most of the chives. Spread on the crostini.
Tear the kale into smaller, crostini-sized pieces and massage a drop of olive oil evenly into each piece.
Layer kale across bread.
Lay the hot egg over the top.
Let the heat wilt the kale.
Garnish with remaining chives, sea salt, and pepper.

Fried Egg OVER ARUGULA

LIKE MANY GREAT THINGS IN MY LIFE, THIS RECIPE CAME FROM MY MOTHER. Until my recent move to Venice, my mom had always lived right down the street from me. Our close proximity wasn't always without complications . . . especially during the time in my life when I yearned for independence and freedom. But after some pretty major fights, we both learned to respect each other's needs and boundaries.

After I grew up a bit, I realized how much I actually needed and wanted my mom close by. And I discovered one great perk: breakfast at Susie's house. I love nothing more than to throw on some sunglasses, glance both ways to make sure the sneaky paparazzi that usually camp out in our neighborhood are nowhere to be found, and dash over to my mom's house in my pajamas. She makes the best coffee (this diva orders her beans from a secret location I don't even get to know about) and is always good for a fried egg over arugula at the last minute.

My favorite thing to do is to show up unannounced. I get a kick out of it, I can't help it. I love the expression on my mom's face as she tries to act annoyed that I just bombarded her morning. I enjoy the slight grin I see in the corner of her mouth and the spark in her eyes as she realizes how important she still is in my adult life.

So while I would love to take credit for creating my favorite breakfast recipe, I can't. It's all Susie's.

SERVES 1

1–2 EGGS
OIL or BUTTER
1 cup ARUGULA
3–5 halved CHERRY TOMATOES
1 tablespoon grated PARMESAN

1 tablespoon EXTRA VIRGIN OLIVE OIL
1 pinch FLAKE SEA SALT and BLACK PEPPER
Squeeze of LEMON

Heat a skillet to medium, add a drop of oil or butter, crack the egg.
Cook until the egg white is firm, but the yellow is still runny.
Combine arugula, cherry tomatoes, parmesan, olive oil, sea salt, black pepper, and lemon in a bowl, then place on a plate.
Lay the warm egg over the greens.
Let the warm, runny yolks wilt and dress the greens.

I SERVED THESE BAKED HERB EGGS WHEN MY GIRLFRIENDS CAME OVER WITH THEIR PUPS, CHAMPAGNE, AND SUNHATS FOR A GIRLS-AND-DOGGIES BRUNCH PARTY. Our dogs ran around together while we flipped through magazines and lounged by the pool. It was such a fun afternoon with the people I love the most!

So many times we plan special meals for the men in our lives, but it's important to remember to do special things for our friends too. The best thing about this brunch? More than likely, you already have most of the ingredients in your kitchen. So round up the ladies, cut some fresh flowers, and throw your own girls' brunch!

SERVES 4

OLIVE OIL
8 EGGS
PARMESAN
¼ cup finely chopped
FLAT-LEAF PARSLEY

¼ cup finely chopped FRESH ROSEMARY
¼ cup finely chopped FRESH THYME
SEA SALT

Preheat the oven to 400 degrees.
Grease the insides of four ramekins with olive oil so the eggs don't stick.
Gently crack two eggs into each dish.
Drizzle with olive oil.
Sprinkle herbs and salt across the top.
Grate some fresh parmesan on top.
Bake until whites are firm.

SERVING SUGGESTION: Pair with crusty bread.

chapter five

I ♥ KALE

"Love" Salad

Breadcrumb and Radish Salad

Sea Salt and Vinegar Kale Chips

Kale, Black Bean, and Butternut Squash Tacos

Raw Beet and Kale Salad

Kale

IF YOU AREN'T FAMILIAR WITH THIS LEAFY GREEN, DON'T STRESS.
By the end of this chapter you will know all kinds of great ways to enjoy it. Living in LA, the land of the health nuts and exercise addicts, I have been eating kale for years. I know I talk about foods that I love all the time, and maybe I use that term a little loosely. I *enjoy* them. I love kale, and I love to introduce it to people who have never come across it before. Once you master kale, you too will have the responsibility of sharing this magical green with new people.

THERE ARE A COUPLE THINGS TO KEEP IN MIND WHEN MAKING KALE RECIPES.

CLEANING KALE:
Fill a large bowl with water. Remove the stems and soak the leaves for 15 minutes. Any hidden dirt will fall to the bottom of the bowl. Lay the kale on towels and let them dry or run through a salad spinner.

MASSAGING KALE:
If you are serving it as a salad, it should always be massaged. Massaging the kale leaves sweetens the kale and helps with digestion.

Once the kale is dry, using a couple drops of olive oil, massage each leaf till they turn bright green. Don't overdo it; just a couple good rubs and you should be good.

STORING KALE:
Unlike other greens, you can store kale, dressed, for up to two days in the refrigerator.

LET'S TALK ABOUT MY LOVE FOR KALE. I know it sounds strange, but I actually crave kale, and it hurts me when I hear people say they don't like it. I get it though—sometimes it's a little earthy or bitter. Kale is the garden's tough guy, but all it takes is a bit of love to see that kale is really a delicate li'l green.

Now this next part may seem a little out there, but just go with me on it, okay? Buddhists believe that praying over your water or meal actually changes the molecular makeup of the food, making it more wholesome and nutritious. Whether or not it works, manifesting love and health never hurt anyone. This "massaged" salad is the perfect opportunity to test out this theory and infuse some positive intention into your food. If you don't buy into it, I won't hold it against you. Regardless, massaging kale isn't just for intention—it aids in the digestion process as well. Kale provides us with tons of antioxidants, flattens our tummies, clears our skin, and is so tasty. If that's not love, I don't know what is.

SERVES 4

2 bunches CURLY KALE
Drizzle of OLIVE OIL
(for massaging the kale)
1 handful quartered CHERRY
TOMATOES
1 handful TOASTED PINE NUTS
(or almonds)
1 handful DRIED CRANBERRIES
(or dried cherries)

Seasoned RICE VINEGAR
LEMON JUICE (to taste)
2 minced cloves GARLIC
1 teaspoon minced SHALLOT
1 tablespoon DIJON MUSTARD
1 tablespoon AGAVE or HONEY
1 generous pinch SEA SALT

Wash and remove the ribs of each piece of kale.
Tear the kale into bite-sized pieces.
Drizzle with olive oil.
Gently massage the oil evenly into each piece.
Add cherry tomatoes, pine nuts, and cranberries.
Toss with dressing.

FOR THE DRESSING:
Combine rice vinegar, lemon juice, minced garlic, minced shallot, Dijon mustard, honey, and sea salt in a mason jar and shake to emulsify.

Breadcrumb AND *Radish* SALAD

BY NOW YOU MAY HAVE NOTICED THAT I USE RADISHES IN A LOT OF MY RECIPES. That's because they are a major superfood. Radishes are filled with antioxidants, fight free radicals, contain a gram of fiber apiece, and only nineteen calories in a half cup! They are great raw or roasted. I love the spice, the color, and the crunch that a radish adds to so many dishes. With all the benefits in a radish, it's no surprise I add them to everything.

SERVES 2

1 bunch TUSCAN KALE
4–5 thinly sliced RADISHES
1 bulb thinly sliced FENNEL
1 cubed AVOCADO
2 tablespoons OLIVE OIL

Juice of 1 small LEMON
1 pinch SEA SALT
2 tablespoons grated PECORINO
1 loaf crusty FRENCH BREAD
or SOURDOUGH

Wash and dry kale and cut into 1-inch pieces.
Massage kale.
Combine with radishes, fennel, and avocado.
Add oil, lemon juice, and salt.
Sprinkle with pecorino and breadcrumbs.

BREADCRUMBS
Let bread dry out for a few days.
Pulse dry bread in a food processor to desired consistency.
Scatter breadcrumbs across a baking sheet.
Broil briefly until browned.

SEA SALT AND VINEGAR *Kale Chips*

EVER SINCE I WAS LITTLE, I HAVE LOVED SEA SALT AND VINEGAR CHIPS. To me, there is nothing better than a great sandwich with sea salt and vinegar chips laid on top of it. I crave that salty kick, and sometimes I NEED it. Unfortunately, along with all that salty goodness, there come loads of sodium, fat, and carbs. These kale chips are a lifesaver when I'm watching my diet. You can come up with different flavors, but this classic one is always a win.

SERVES 2

1 bunch CURLY KALE	1 tablespoon OLIVE OIL
2 tablespoons WHITE VINEGAR	1 teaspoon SEA SALT

Wash and dry kale very thoroughly (the drier the kale, the crunchier the chip).
Tear the kale into bite-sized pieces.
In a mixing bowl, toss the kale with the vinegar until fully coated.
Lay the kale out to dry on a baking sheet covered with aluminum foil.
Once the vinegar has dried, spray olive oil across the kale and sprinkle with sea salt.
Bake at 350 degrees for 5–10 minutes.
Check the kale every few minutes.
Remove any pieces that are turning color more quickly than the rest.

Note: An olive oil sprayer works wonders for this recipe. It keeps the olive oil from getting too heavy on each piece. The lighter the coating, the crunchier the kale. So if you have a sprayer, now is the time to use it!

- 4 leaves CURLY KALE
- Drizzle of OLIVE OIL
- 1 ear SWEET CORN
- 1 can low-sodium BLACK BEANS
- 1 chopped JALAPEÑO

Small CORN TORTILLAS
2 cups cubed and roasted
BUTTERNUT SQUASH
CASHEW CHEESE
HABANERO HOT SAUCE

Massage kale with a drizzle of olive oil.

Boil the corn and cut it from the cob.

Sauté the corn, black beans, and jalepeño in a skillet on medium heat.

Sprinkle the mixture with a generous pinch of sea salt.

Warm the tortillas between two paper towels in the microwave.

Layer the tortillas with the kale, corn mixture, and butternut squash.

Drizzle with cashew cheese.

Add a few drops of hot sauce.

Sprinkle with sea salt.

IF CASHEW CHEESE DOESN'T SOUND LIKE YOUR CUP OF TEA, SUBSTITUTE WITH SOME SHREDDED CHEDDAR. I SUGGEST GIVING IT A TRY, THOUGH. I THINK YOU MIGHT BE SURPRISED!

I MET MY FRIEND BRITTANY WHILE SHOOTING *ALL ABOUT CHRISTMAS EVE* FOR LIFETIME. (Sidenote: I love a good Lifetime movie. There is nothing better than watching a Lifetime thriller on a Sunday afternoon while nursing a hangover!) Britt was in the wardrobe department, and we first met at my fitting. I had twenty-seven costume changes, so needless to say she and the costume designer had their work cut out for them. One by one we chose outfits and sent the pictures off to the producers. I loved her right away and could tell we would be friends. She is open, easygoing, hardworking, and driven. She is also only twenty-four years old (did I mention that?) and really has her shit together—even more than some of my friends in their thirties.

This movie was a special experience for me because I was also working with my friend Ashley, who has been my makeup artist for years. During the filming, Ashley, Britt, two of the production assistants, and I developed a group we call "The Divas." We became instant best friends, and each of us dons a specific diva nickname. (I was dubbed "Undercover Diva," and I'll never tell you why.) We drove everybody nuts with our BFF behavior. We had sleepovers, took a wild weekend away, and even got tattoos together. We had a slogan ("Sorry we're not sorry"), and I'm pretty sure we were the only ones who thought it was funny. During one of our sleepovers, we discovered these kale and black bean tacos with habanero hot sauce. In this updated version, I added the butternut squash and corn, but no matter what, we never skimp on the hot sauce.

These tacos require a couple of steps, but don't get intimidated! They are actually quite simple.

CASHEW CHEESE

1 cup CASHEWS	1/2 cup NUTRITIONAL YEAST
2 tablespoons CHIPOTLE PEPPERS IN ADOBO SAUCE	1 cup AGAR FLAKES
	2 tablespoons ONION POWDER
2 tablespoons LEMON JUICE	2 tablespoons GARLIC POWDER

Soak the cashews in water overnight until plump.

Drain.

Blend cashews, adobo sauce, lemon juice, nutritional yeast, agar flakes, onion powder, and garlic powder in a Vitamix, high-powered blender, or food processor until smooth.

Raw Beet AND Kale SALAD

THIS SALAD REMINDS ME OF MY FRIEND HANNAH. We met through mutual friends last year at Coachella Music Festival but really only got to know each other after I'd moved to Venice. We bumped into each other at a nail salon and planned a workout for the next day. That workout was followed up with a lunch, and pretty soon we made this a regular routine. Hannah loves food the way I do, is a great workout motivator, and inspires me to make healthy choices. She is the most generous and thoughtful friend, and you can't help but want to save the world when you are with her.

SERVES 1-2

1 bunch CURLY KALE
1 peeled GOLDEN BEET
1 sliced CARROT

1 cubed AVOCADO
LEMON TAHINI DRESSING
(page 190)

Wash the kale, remove ribs, tear into bite-sized pieces, and massage.

Grate the beet and carrot into a bowl.

Add the avocado.

Toss with Lemon Tahini Dressing.

WHENEVER I POST A BEET RECIPE ON REAL GIRL'S KITCHEN, I GET SUCH AN ASSORTED ARRAY OF COMMENTS. PEOPLE EITHER LOVE THEM OR HATE THEM. I HAPPEN TO THINK THEY ARE FANTASTIC, BUT I CAN UNDERSTAND THE SLIGHT FRUSTRATION THAT COMES ALONG WITH THEM. THEY ARE AN INGREDIENT THAT REQUIRES MULTIPLE STEPS, AND MY FINGERS ARE ALL TOO FAMILIAR WITH THE MAGENTA DYE JOB THAT THEY LEAVE BEHIND. I LOVE THEM, SO I AM HAPPY TO ROCK HOT PINK FINGERS FOR THE REST OF THE DAY. IF YOU AREN'T SO KEEN ON THAT LOOK, AVOID THE ROASTING AND TRY THEM RAW. THEY GIVE A GREAT CRUNCH TO THE SALAD, A HINT OF SWEETNESS, AND A WHOLE LOT OF HEALTH BENEFITS. THEY ARE FILLED WITH FIBER AND HELP TO OXYGENATE YOUR BLOOD, WHICH GIVES YOU ENERGY. THEY ALSO AID IN CLEANSING YOUR LIVER.

Lemon
Tahini

chapter six
SOUPS

Chipotle Tomato Soup

Corn Chowder

Watermelon Gazpacho

Spicy Chicken Noodle "Sick" Soup

Shrimp, White Bean, and Kale "Heartbreak" Soup

Chipotle Tomato SOUP

NO TWO THINGS IN THE WORLD GO TOGETHER BETTER THAN TOMATO SOUP AND GRILLED CHEESE, EXCEPT FOR ONE OF MY LONGTIME FRIENDS, DREW, AND ME. We met when I was seventeen years old and he was working for a clothing line that was generous enough to gift me with some new outfits. I went to the fitting and in walked a tall, red-haired, fabulous gay man. He was wearing a diva attitude, a maroon bouffant, and a lightning-bolt necklace nestled under a skinny red necktie. We were destined to be best friends.

A few years later, I was living in New York and didn't have many friends yet. Drew came to the rescue and spent a little over a week with me to show me the ropes. We found all kinds of great restaurants together, but our favorite was a tiny place called Say Cheese, which only served tomato soup and grilled cheese. The decor looked like something you would find in a preschool: small colorful tables that sat low to the ground, puzzle-piece rugs, and a chalkboard menu. It was like being a kid all over again.

One rainy day, we decided that nothing would satisfy our hunger like Say Cheese, and we had to have it. We pulled on our rain boots, grabbed our umbrellas, and started the treacherous walk over there. I say that because by the time we got there, the bottom halves of our clothes were soaked, and the wind had flipped both of our umbrellas inside out. We looked like drowned rats, but it was worth it. We have been back to Say Cheese many times together over the past few years, but our rain-soaked afternoon will always be my favorite.

7 quartered TOMATOES
2 quartered YELLOW ONIONS
Drizzle of OLIVE OIL
1 tablespoon SEA SALT
1 cup VEGETABLE STOCK
1 can CRUSHED TOMATOES
1/2 cup RED WINE

4 heads ROASTED GARLIC (page 175)
2 RED BELL PEPPERS, quartered
and seeds removed
1 teaspoon BLACK PEPPER
1 cup torn BASIL
1/4 cup CHIPOTLE PEPPERS
IN ADOBO SAUCE

Preheat the oven to 350 degrees.

Drizzle the tomatoes and onions with olive oil.

Sprinkle with salt.

Bake for 30 minutes or until soft and sunken.

Combine vegetable stock, crushed tomatoes, and red wine in a pot.

Bring to a slow boil.

Add tomatoes, onions, garlic, red peppers, black pepper, basil, and chipotle adobo sauce.

Let simmer for about an hour.

Run the soup through a food mill, Vitamix, or emulsion blender.

BEST SERVED WITH GRILLED CHEESE SANDWICHES.

Corn Chowder

I MADE THIS SOUP FOR A GROUP OF FRIENDS AT THE FIRST SIGN OF FALL. I was experimenting with recipe ideas when a serious craving for soup hit me. Corn season at the farmer's market was slowly coming to an end, and I wanted to make one more great corn recipe before it was over. It was finally chilly enough to put on a sweater, and when I texted friends to ask if anyone felt like coming over for soup, everyone's response was an enthusiastic yes. Pretty soon my kitchen was filled with a handful of my closest friends. We all gathered around the table and shared the details of our days over a big bowl of soup, a mixed green salad, and some crusty bread to dunk into our bowls. It was a relaxed and simple night, my favorite kind.

ERVES 4

4 ears CORN
1 tablespoon EARTH BALANCE or BUTTER
1 chopped ONION
6 strips BACON, chopped
2 peeled and chopped POTATOES

1 chopped and deseeded RED BELL PEPPER
2 cups WATER
1/4 cup HALF-AND-HALF
1 4-oz. can GREEN CHILIES
KOSHER SALT and BLACK PEPPER

Cut the kernels from each ear of corn.
Warm the butter in a big pot.
Add the onion and bacon.
When the bacon is almost done, add the chopped potatoes and red bell pepper.
Add water and bring to a boil.
Once the potatoes are soft, add corn, half-and-half, chilies, salt, and pepper.

You can enjoy this soup a couple of ways. You can leave it chunky, or you can run it through a food mill. While I prefer a food mill, you can also blend it in a Vitamix or use a handheld emulsion blender.

Watermelon Gazpacho

GAZPACHO ALWAYS REMINDS ME OF MY GRANDFATHER. He lived in Laguna Niguel, California, and whenever we went to visit him, he always made us gazpacho. His house was nothing short of amazing: It had an indoor pool, a painting studio, a big koi pond, and lots of lush, tropical gardens for us to day-dream in. We loved playing make-believe in his house and creating all kinds of great adventures. Usually they would involve some kind of secret mission that required us getting from one end of his house to the other without being spotted by my mom or grandfather.

These memories make me so grateful that I grew up at a time when kids still played outside. I think that's one of the reasons my sister and I have always been so close. We never played video games for hours on end, and the TV was never our babysitter. Our after-school activities usually consisted of making up dances to our favorite songs, bike rides, playing basketball in the driveway, or taking night swims with our family. We didn't spend our time on iChat with friends or texting at the dinner table; we spent our time dreaming with each other.

SERVES 2

1 cubed seedless WATERMELON
2 chopped large HEIRLOOM TOMATOES
1 clove pressed GARLIC
1/2 finely chopped WHITE ONION
1/2 chopped GREEN ONION
1 chopped CUCUMBER

Juice of 1 LIME
1 handful chopped CILANTRO
1/2 deseeded JALAPEÑO
1 teaspoon SEA SALT
1 teaspoon BLACK PEPPER
GOAT CHEESE to garnish

• •

Place all ingredients in a Vitamix or blender.
Pulse a few times, but don't overblend.
Pour into a bowl and garnish with goat cheese.

NOTE: I like my gazpacho chunky, so I set aside half the watermelon, to-mato, and cucumber and stir them back in once I've blended the rest.

THIS SOUP FIRST CAME INTO ROTATION WHILE MY SISTER WAS ON A US TOUR. She had a concert almost every night and had been working like crazy for months. The minute she got home and actually had a chance to relax, she got sick. This was a pretty regular occurrence for a couple of years. I started making her this soup to clear her nose and throat, and pretty soon she started asking me to make it even when she wasn't sick. It is very spicy but very delicious and is the best cure for a stuffy nose.

This recipe makes a big batch, which is great for when you're sick. Who feels like cooking twice? Save what you don't eat, and it will be even better the next day.

SERVES 4

8 cups **CHICKEN BROTH**
2 cups **WATER**
1 cup **ORZO** or **BROWN RICE**
2 cups chopped, cooked **CHICKEN BREAST**
1 cup chopped **CARROTS**
1 cup chopped **CELERY**
1 chopped **YELLOW ONION**

4 peeled cloves **GARLIC**
1 **JALAPEÑO** (I let a couple seeds fall into the pot for added heat)
2 handfuls chopped **CILANTRO**
1 teaspoon **KOSHER SALT**
1 tablespoon **GROUND PEPPER**
CRUSHED RED PEPPER to taste

Bring chicken broth and water to a boil.
Add orzo.
Add chicken, veggies, garlic (whole or pressed), and deseeded jalapeño.
After a few minutes, lower heat.
Add cilantro and simmer until ready to eat.
Add salt, pepper, and crushed red pepper.

NOTE: Orzo is a small pasta that looks like rice.

ONE THING I'VE LEARNED IS THAT THERE IS NO MANUAL ON HOW TO DEAL WITH A BREAKUP. No matter who pulls the trigger, both parties are left reeling. My last breakup was no exception.

It took me a while to see that it wasn't working, but once I did there was no closing my eyes. One day, after a short bike ride, I came home and ended one of the most significant relationships in my life. Just like that, it was done, as if all the mighty forces (I totally credit my angels for this one) came together and carried me through it. The words came out of my mouth effortlessly and without tears. I was standing in the middle of one of those "only you can change your life" moments and I felt empowered. I was high on my own adrenaline and feeling like myself for the first time in a while.

Well, that feeling lasted about twenty-four hours.

Then fear and heartache set in. I finally broke the news to my family and my girlfriends, and shortly after, all of my real-life angels rallied around me. The love and unity I felt during that time is something I will never forget. I can remember looking around my kitchen, seeing my sister and the faces of some of my longtime girlfriends, and thinking, *These are the faces I hope I see when I'm old.* They think I don't know, but they each pulled shifts. One would spend the night with me, and as she would leave, another would arrive. They went through the whole process with me, and I am eternally grateful.

I had always heard about people who "couldn't eat" after a traumatic experience, but I was never one of them. I was the girl who was all too happy to eat a bowl of mac and cheese in the midst of a crisis. But this time was different. For two weeks, I had no appetite. When I was finally hungry, I craved soup. I wanted something hearty and warm. Something that felt like it was going to hug me from the inside out. This soup was the first thing I ate, and I ate it exclusively for about four days. It's cozy like a favorite sweater, and it brings me back to a time when I was fragile and strong all at once.

4 cloves GARLIC
10 deveined SHRIMP
1 tablespoon SEA SALT
BLACK PEPPER to taste
2 cans CRUSHED TOMATOES
1 cup WATER
1 can CHICKEN BROTH

10 leaves chopped KALE
1 diced large ZUCCHINI
1 deseeded JALAPEÑO
CAYENNE to taste
PAPRIKA to taste
LEMON JUICE to taste
2 15-oz.cans CANNELLINI BEANS

Peel the garlic cloves and drop them in a pot whole.

Season the shrimp with salt and pepper.

Grill in a pan, browning both sides of the shrimp, and set aside.

Bring tomatoes, water, and chicken broth to a boil with the garlic.

Add all of the remaining ingredients, except the shrimp and one can of cannellini beans.

Blend the remaining can of beans in a food processor until chunky. This will add some nice texture to the soup.

Add beans to pot.

Simmer for 1–2 hours.

When you are ready to serve, add a couple of shrimp to each bowl.

Heart healed.

NOTE: I love to save any leftover soup in a large mason jar. It's always better the next day.

chapter seven
APPS
AND
SNACKS

Bacon-Wrapped Dates

Sausage and Thyme Stuffed Mushrooms

Hummus

Mushroom and Herb Crostini

Asparagus and Prosciutto Crescent Rolls

Burrata and Sun-Dried Tomatoes

Baked Buffalo Wings

MANY OF MY FAVORITE CHILDHOOD MEMORIES INVOLVE BACON. In fact, I'm probably still working off some of the bacon I ate as a child. As proud Texans, we wrapped everything in bacon. Bacon-wrapped chicken, quail, shrimp, and even veggies were (and still are) a staple in our home.

My dad recently came to visit me in Los Angeles, and instead of going out somewhere fancy, I wanted to cook us dinner. We don't see each other as often as we would like, and I think he was a little nervous for me to be at the helm in the kitchen. He remembers the days when I burned everything I touched and even blew up a couple of microwaves. Needless to say, he had every right to be nervous.

My dad complains about the wimpy health food in Los Angeles, so I knew that for this dinner, my healthy staples wouldn't do. I needed something special. Something that would really pop. Something that would impress my good ol' pops and make him proud. Then I remembered bacon.

Knowing that I could never grill a piece of meat the way my dad can, I decided to make my own version of a family classic. Instead of wrapping pieces of chicken, I wrapped up dates. If you have never baked dates, I suggest you get on it ASAP. They come out of the oven like gooey pieces of candy. Add a bit of blue cheese in the center and wrap some bacon around them, and you will never be the same.

Even after all these years and the mounds of kale, seaweed, and quinoa that have infiltrated my diet, one thing will never change: my love for bacon and anything that's wrapped up in it.

YIELD: 24 DATES

1/2 cup **BLUE CHEESE**	24 **DATES**
2 tablespoons **HEAVY WHIPPING CREAM**	1 pound (12 slices) **THICK-CUT BACON**
	TOOTHPICKS

Bring the blue cheese to room temperature.

Preheat the oven to 400 degrees.

Slice dates lengthwise 3/4 of the way down.

In a small bowl, press the cream into the blue cheese with a fork.

Press a small scoop of the blue cheese into the center of the dates and close them back up.

Cut each piece of bacon in half.

Wrap each halved bacon strip around a date.

Secure with a toothpick.

Place bacon-wrapped dates on a baking sheet.

Bake for 15–20 minutes.

VEGETARIAN? NOT TO WORRY! YOU CAN STILL ENJOY THESE SINFUL LITTLE SNACKS. SKIP THE BACON AND MIX SOME CRUSHED WALNUTS INTO THE BLUE CHEESE MIXTURE. BAKE IN A 350-DEGREE OVEN FOR 10 MINUTES.

I COULDN'T GET THESE DATES TO PHOTOGRAPH WELL, SO I CALLED MY FRIEND TYLER. BACON-WRAPPED DATES NEVER LOOKED SO . . . HANDSOME.

BUTTON MUSHROOMS,
large enough for stuffing
1 link SAUSAGE
1 deseeded JALAPEÑO
1 cup grated PECORINO

1 cup grated PARMESAN
1 EGG YOLK
1 tablespoon chopped THYME
1–2 teaspoons LEMON JUICE

Preheat the oven to 350 degrees.

Wipe each mushroom with a wet dishtowel to remove any dirt.

Pull out each stem and set aside.

Remove the casing from the sausage.

Heat sausage in a skillet over medium heat, until it starts to break apart, then remove from pan.

Finely chop the mushroom stems and jalapeño.

Combine sausage, mushroom stems, jalapeño, cheese, yolk, thyme, and lemon juice in a mixing bowl.

Place mushrooms on a baking sheet covered in aluminum foil.

Stuff each mushroom with mixture.

Bake for 20 minutes.

WHEN I WAS EIGHTEEN, I BRIEFLY DATED THIS GUY WHO HAS SINCE RESURFACED IN MY LIFE. He is smart, handsome, and loves things like painting, sailing, sculpting, cooking, drinking great wine, and playing the piano.

We met on the set of a short-lived television series, and I played his girlfriend for a couple of episodes. Around Christmas, I mentioned that I'd never experienced a white Christmas. A couple of weeks later, he threw a Christmas party at his house and had a company come out to blow snow all over his yard and across the top of his house. It was unlike anything I had ever seen. Kids in his Los Angeles neighborhood were making snowmen in the middle of December. He is full of grand gestures, and to say this man is a romantic is a vast understatement. Being a silly eighteen-year-old who still needed some life experience, I wasn't mature enough to appreciate all the sweet things he did for me, and we decided it was best to just be friends. Time went by, and we both went on to date other people.

Years later, I moved to his neighborhood and thought I would just send him a quick "hello" text. He responded immediately, and even better, he responded with a phone call. A PHONE CALL. I couldn't believe it. Guys never call anymore, but of course he did. He asked me out for dinner, and a couple of days later there we were, sitting across from one another over a great bottle of wine. The strange part was that it felt like no time had passed.

For one of our next dates, he suggested we take a cooking class together. We made five different fall hors d'oeuvres and had the best time.

After dating a string of selfish guys and lazy boys, he was so refreshing, and I feel lucky to have his friendship.

Hummus

IF YOU CAN'T ALREADY TELL, I'M A HOPELESS ROMANTIC. I love to be in love and I live for love affairs. This past year I was working on a film, and I found myself in an organic vegetable love affair. That sounds much dirtier than it was. Before you roll your eyes, let me explain.

One day on set, a guy struck up a conversation with me about my blog. He explained that he too loved to cook and he actually had a pretty impressive garden. I was instantly intrigued. I had been single for almost a year and found him to be a breath of fresh California air. He has this incredible sun-kissed, long blond hair, a flawless tan, and piercing (but kind) ocean-blue eyes. On top of the fact that he was one of the most handsome men I have ever met, he was funny. We instantly started sharing stories of our favorite dishes, and it was pretty clear to everyone around us that there was some serious chemistry popping off.

He had told me he loved hummus, and I happen to have a pretty solid recipe. I went home, made him a batch of hummus, and shot him a message saying to come find me at my trailer because I was bringing him a surprise. When I opened my trailer door I was greeted by bags of home-grown kale, heirloom tomatoes, cucumbers, bell peppers, carrots, and arugula. All from his garden. The whole trailer was filled with an earthy, fresh aroma, and in that moment I knew this was the beginning of a culinary romance. As he tried the hummus a smile slid across his face, and I knew I had done a good job.

Some love affairs don't always last forever. However, this one was special. He came along at the perfect time in my life. He showed me that even though I had been let down by someone in the past, there were still great guys out there. Turns out he wasn't *my* guy, but he was one of the good ones, and I always think fondly of him every time I make this recipe.

SERVES 1-2

2 cans CHICKPEAS, drained and rinsed	2 tablespoons TAHINI
1/4 cup PINE NUTS	2 overflowing tablespoons OLIVE OIL
6 cloves GARLIC	Juice of half a LEMON
1 cup FAGE 0% FAT GREEK YOGURT	Generous pinch SEA SALT
	Generous pinch CAYENNE PEPPER
	1 teaspoon PAPRIKA

Blend all ingredients in a food processor or Vitamix. Garnish with a drizzle of olive oil, a couple pine nuts, and a sprinkle of paprika.

Mushroom AND Herb Crostini

A COUPLE OF YEARS AGO, I MADE THESE CROSTINI FOR A DINNER PARTY AT MY HOUSE. As most of my dinner parties go, I got a call from two of my guests at the last minute asking to bring a plus-one. I know some people hate stuff like that, but I always think the more, the merrier. (I *don't* like when people ask who else is invited, but that's beside the point!) Anyway, I found myself a little short on food, and these were a last-minute addition to my menu. They came out great, and to my surprise, they were the biggest hit of the night.

This is my original version, but feel free to play with ingredients too! Add some peppers, use a different kind of cheese, or experiment with spices. You really can't go wrong with these.

YIELD: 2 DOZEN CROSTINI

CRUSTY FRENCH BAGUETTE, cut into 24 slices	5 cups BUTTON MUSHROOMS (or a mushroom mix)
½ cup OLIVE OIL	1/2 cup WHITE WINE
1/4 cup grated GRUYÈRE	1 tablespoon TAMARI
1 tablespoon EARTH BALANCE or BUTTER	1/4 cup chopped CHIVES
A pinch of SEA SALT	1/4 cup chopped flat-leaf PARSLEY

Preheat the oven to 400 degrees.

Brush both sides of each baguette slice lightly with olive oil.

Bake for 4 minutes per side.

Remove from the oven and sprinkle with gruyère.

Place the crostini back in the oven under the broiler until the cheese is melted.

Melt Earth Balance or butter in a medium-heat skillet.

Add mushrooms, white wine, and tamari.

Cook until mushrooms are soft and liquid has evaporated.

Finish with a small pinch of sea salt.

Spoon mushrooms out of the pan directly onto crostini.

Garnish with chopped chives and flat-leaf parsley.

NOTE: Truffle oil is also a great addition. Simply drizzle across the top of the crostini once plated.

WITHOUT GETTING TOO SAPPY, I'M GOING TO TELL YOU ABOUT MY MOM. We call her Susie, and she is the best. Yes, she can drive me crazy. Yes, I can royally piss her off. But at the end of the day, she is my ride-or-die chick.

Susie was the mom who loved to get up early and drive my carpool. She was the mom who packed a homemade lunch every single day and always included a happy note. She was the mom who was excited to take my friends and me to toilet-paper a boy's house on a Saturday night. Then she would take us all for doughnuts on Sunday, and she'd help us clean it up afterward. She cooked dinner almost every night, and on many occasions she could be found up on the kitchen counter with a wooden spoon, belting out the oldies. She helped me deal with mean girls in middle school and cried with me over my first heartbreak. She was the first person to ever wax my eyebrows and the one who yelled at me the first time I helped my sister shave her legs without permission. She was a total blast to grow up with, and she's someone I'm happy to know as an adult. She taught me how to stand up for myself, how to be a lady, and (last but not least) how to cook.

One thing I always remember my mom making is pigs-in-a-blanket. She used to make them every morning when I had friends sleep over, and she got quite the reputation. Looking back, I feel bad for some of the other parents—everybody wants to be the favorite house for sleepovers. You know, the house with the best snacks and the best area to make an indoor fort. Well, my mom was steep competition.

Here is my updated version of Susie's classic.

YIELD: 6 PIGS-IN-A-BLANKET

1 dozen **ASPARAGUS** spears	1 package **PILLSBURY**
1/2 cup grated **ASIAGO**	**CRESCENT ROLLS**
6 slices **PROSCIUTTO**	

Preheat the oven to 375 degrees.

Roll 2 asparagus spears, a pinch of asiago, and a piece of prosciutto into each crescent roll.

Bake for 10–12 minutes or until golden brown.

NOTE: If I'm serving these at a party, I love to drizzle honey across the top. Also, after reading my mom this story, she asked me to read this at her funeral. Whatever you want, Mom. Whatever you want.

WHEN I WAS EIGHTEEN, MY GIRLFRIENDS AND I DECIDED TO START A GIRLS' NIGHT ONCE A WEEK. It gave us a chance to get together and take a much-needed break from boyfriends and school. Having this time together strengthened our relationships with each other, and years later, I'm still close with most of the original "girls' night" attendees.

We've been through a lot together, from breakups to family drama to issues that plague so many young girls, like our relationships with food. It shocks me when I hear women say that they don't have any girlfriends or that they don't get along with other women. My friendships with women have been some of the most fulfilling and supportive relationships in my life.

Some eight years later, our dinners are still going strong. Some of us are single, some are married, and some are in serious relationships. No matter what, our favorite topic is always sex. On the night I made this burrata appetizer, the group got particularly rowdy. We made a big spread of food and sat around snacking and laughing on the floor of my living room. Almost immediately, the dirty talk commenced, and we started sharing stories of our latest sexcapades. At one point during the night, we stole the phone of one of the girls and sexted with her crush, pretending to be her. Later that night, he showed up at her front door, professed his love for her, and proceeded to knock her socks off.

We all love to remind her of our group's effort that night and its very fruitful payoff. I still stand by the idea that she should have sent us all flowers the next day. It just goes to show you: sometimes it takes a village.

SERVES 2

ASPARAGUS TIPS
Approx. 2 tablespoons OLIVE OIL
A pinch of SEA SALT
ARUGULA
LEMON JUICE, to taste

SUN-DRIED TOMATOES
A handful of toasted PINE NUTS
1 BURRATA CHEESE BALL
A generous stack of your favorite CRACKERS

Drop the asparagus tips into a large pot of boiling water for 1 minute.
Remove from heat and immediately dunk into a bowl of ice water. (This is called blanching. It brightens the color, softens the texture, and destroys enzymes, which keeps vegetables fresher longer.)
Once cool, toss in a drizzle of olive oil and sea salt.
Toss arugula in a drizzle of olive oil and a splash of lemon juice and arrange on a plate.
Lay the burrata, asparagus tips, sun-dried tomatoes, and toasted pine nuts over the arugula.
Serve with crackers.

Baked Buffalo Wings

I SPENT THE SUMMER I GOT MY DRIVER'S LICENSE IN TEXAS, WITH MY DAD. My dad is a Texas man. He hunts, makes the world's greatest steak, can fix anything, and loves to take me out . . . for buffalo wings. And not just any buffalo wings. The wings from Hooters. Yes, Hooters.

On one of our driving lessons we passed by a local outpost, and I made some snarky comment about the place. I should have kept my comments to myself, because my dad immediately told me to pull in and that we were stopping for lunch. I wanted to die, but to be honest, I was hungry. We grabbed a seat at one of the high barstool tables and ordered a big plate of wings. I have to admit, they were crispy, spicy, and just plain fantastic. My dad has always gotten a kick out of trying to embarrass me, and this time was no different. So of course he made friends with everyone in that place, and I even left with a T-shirt. Little did he know that I had a plan to get him back!

I need to tell you about my first car. It was a 1984 beige Suburban with a turquoise stripe running down both sides. Someone had obviously been using the fabric seats as a place to wipe their fast-food fingers, and the way back had been converted to fit a wheelchair lift. I don't know where on earth my dad found this thing, but he thought driving it would build my character, and if I got into a fender bender, well, I would be okay. I spent weeks trying to figure out how to ditch this ride. Should I run into something? Should I leave it unlocked somewhere with the keys on the seat and act clueless when it turned up stolen? The truth was, I would have had to pay someone to take it off my hands. But then, walking out of Hooters . . . it hit me.

The conversation went something like this:

"Dad, I know I've been complaining about the Suburban, but I really do appreciate it. Some kids don't get their own car. Thank you."

"Haylie, I'm happy for you to have it. You have really become a great driver, and I'm so proud of you. Can I ask, why the change of heart?"

"Well, I think I can fit a full-sized bed in the back."

My dad almost choked on his to-go cup of iced tea. I was doing everything I could to keep a straight face. I'm not exaggerating when I tell you that the Suburban was gone the next day. He ended up buying my mom a new car, and I took her old one. I finally confessed my brilliant maneuver a few years later, and we had a big laugh. My dad and I still love to eat wings together, and when we do, we usually share a little sideways glance, both remembering that afternoon.

10 chicken WINGS
1 teaspoon PAPRIKA

1 teaspoon CAYENNE
½ cup FRANK'S REDHOT SAUCE

• •

Preheat the oven to 400 degrees.

Wash and thoroughly dry each wing (you want them dry so the skin gets crispy).

Season each piece with paprika and cayenne.

Place them on a cookie cooling rack and put a baking pan underneath the rack (the rack will help to avoid steaming them, and the sheet underneath will catch any drippings).

Bake for 6–7 minutes.

Remove from the oven and coat each piece with Frank's RedHot.

Bake for another 2–3 minutes, remove from the oven, and serve.

chapter eight
VEGETABLES

Lime and Cotija Corn

Artichoke, Cauliflower, and Pea Gratin

Dijon Brussels Sprouts

Pecorino and Red Pepper Broccolini

Sweet and Spicy Butternut Squash

Lime AND Cotija Corn

THIS CORN RECIPE WAS INSPIRED BY ONE OF MY ALL-TIME FAVORITE PLACES TO EAT IN NEW YORK, CAFE HABANA.

The summer of 2006 was filled with a lot of firsts for me. I moved to New York City, was living alone for the first time, was acting in a Broadway play, and was discovering the neighborhoods of a new city by myself. And when I say "discovering," I mean I got lost a lot. One Sunday afternoon, I had just finished a matinee show and decided to hop in a cab to SoHo, a neighborhood I wasn't too familiar with. I am at my happiest exploring new places with no agenda, and I love to play what I call "Stranger in a Strange Land." But when I was ready to head back home, I learned something the hard way. The cabdrivers change shifts between three PM and five PM, and all the cabs report back to their garages. It is next to impossible to get a ride during these hours, and unless you are a true New Yorker, no one tells you these things.

So with time to kill and a growing appetite, I started looking for some place to hole up. I rounded the corner of Prince and Elizabeth Streets and landed in front of Cafe Habana in all its tiny, delicious, Cuban glory. I grabbed a seat at the bar and took note of what other people were ordering. I find that to be the best way to get the good stuff. Each table had heaping mounds of gnawed corncobs and limes that had had the life squeezed out of them. So clearly I was ordering the corn.

What arrived in front of me in the next few minutes will hold a place in my culinary heart forever. Corn on the cob, charred from a well-seasoned BBQ, a thin layer of mayonnaise painted down the sides, rolled in shredded cotija cheese, with a light sprinkling of their special spice mix and a heavy dose of lime. It is absolute heaven. My lips and fingertips were on fire by the end of the meal, but it was a pain I was all too happy to endure.

Now, I don't make a trip to New York without visiting Cafe Habana. We have good memories together. I had one of the best kisses of my life sitting in their front window on a warm New York night. I holed up there for a couple of hours in the middle of one of the worst blizzards New York had ever seen. I have eaten there dripping with sweat in the blaring heat of July and have taken refuge there many times on a rainy day. I can't help but remember being that girl, terrified of the big city and falling in love with it all at the same time. Even after all these years I'll still take that corn any way I can get it. It always comes back to the corn.

2 ears CORN
1 tablespoon OLIVE OIL
1 tablespoon MAYONNAISE

1 pinch CAYENNE
Finely grated COTIJA to taste
1 big LIME wedge

Husk the corn and slice off kernels using a sharp knife.

Heat a skillet to medium-high heat.

Once hot, add olive oil and corn.

When the kernels become a toasty color, add the mayonnaise, cayenne, and cotija.
Mix well.

Remove from heat and add a big squeeze of lime.

THIS CORN RECIPE IS ALSO GREAT FOR THE GRILL

Peel back the husks, but don't remove them.

Paint on olive oil, mayonnaise, cayenne, and cotija.

Wrap the husks back up around the corn, and throw these babies on the grill.

Artichoke, Cauliflower, AND Pea Gratin

AS YOU CAN PROBABLY TELL, I DON'T USE FROZEN VEGETABLES VERY OFTEN. For me, cooking is about the whole experience. I enjoy browsing the grocery store or farmer's market, looking for food inspiration. I like seeing the familiar faces at the checkout line. I like picking out the perfect pot or pan to prepare my meal in, and I even like cleaning the vegetables before I cook them. With just a subtle shift of your perception, I think there can be something a little romantic about it.

Sometimes I just don't have it in me to steam dozens of artichokes just to get to the hearts. Luckily, a frozen bag of artichoke hearts is exactly what is called for in this recipe. There have been multiple studies over the least few years stating that frozen vegetables might actually be better for us. They say that the enzymes die as the vegetable sits on the shelf but remain intact when they are frozen. So make no apologies for choosing the quick way!

SERVES 4-6

1-pound bag FROZEN ARTICHOKE HEARTS
1 pound chopped CAULIFLOWER
1-pound bag FROZEN PEAS
2 cups low-fat MILK
1/2 stick BUTTER
2 tablespoons FLOUR
1 teaspoon NUTMEG

1/2 teaspoon CHILI POWDER
1/2 teaspoon CRUSHED RED PEPPER
1/2 teaspoon SEA SALT
1/2 teaspoon BLACK PEPPER
1 tablespoon chopped THYME, separated (1/2 to garnish)
1-1/4 cup grated PARMESAN, divided (1/4 cup for topping)

Preheat the oven to 400 degrees.

Drop artichoke hearts and cauliflower into a pot of boiling water for 1–2 minutes, just long enough to soften.

Add the peas for the last minute. Drain.

Bring milk and butter to a slow boil in an oven-safe skillet.

Add flour and seasonings.

Whisk until no clumps remain.

Add 1 cup of parmesan and stir.

Fold the cauliflower, artichokes, and peas into the mixture.

Bake for 15 minutes and remove from oven.

Sprinkle remaining 1/4 cup of parmesan across the top.

Place back in the oven and let the parmesan melt.

Garnish with thyme.

Dijon BRUSSELS SPROUTS

POOR BRUSSELS SPROUTS! SO MANY PEOPLE SAY THEY DON'T LIKE THEM. I think it's because we were forced to eat them as children. I can remember negotiations with my grandmother to eat at least three before excusing myself from the table. Those three brussels sprouts would usually end up tucked inside one of my pockets, only to be discovered once they had been through the rinse cycle.

Now that I'm all grown up, brussels sprouts have become one of my favorite veggies. When I first met my boyfriend, he didn't eat anything green. I was shocked! No salad? No vegetables? Knowing that I am a brussels sprouts master, I made these one night in an attempt to get him to like vegetables. He loved the crispy leaves and has even been known to eat them cold the next day. In fact, he now requests these on a weekly basis.

While brussels sprouts are often paired with bacon or pancetta, I love this Dijon version! It's vegetarian, healthier, and every bit as tasty.

SERVES 2

20 halved BRUSSELS SPROUTS	SEA SALT
2 tablespoons OLIVE OIL	2 tablespoons DIJON MUSTARD

Preheat the oven to 350 degrees.

Toss brussels sprouts with olive oil.

Arrange on baking sheet with centers facing up.

Sprinkle with sea salt.

Bake for 30 minutes or until desired tenderness (I like mine a bit charred).

Remove from heat and toss sprouts in Dijon mustard.

Serve.

NOTE: This is a great dish for dinner parties. It can be made ahead of time, and you score major points for serving brussels sprouts that people actually like.

Pecorino AND *Red Pepper* Broccolini

I HAVE NEVER BEEN A FAN OF BROCCOLI. It gives me flashbacks of my childhood and being encouraged to eat it raw, dipped in ranch dressing, or, even worse, steamed. (Shudder.) So when *broccolini* appeared in supermarkets, I was wary but intrigued. It's like good old-fashioned broccoli, but with a subtle hint of asparagus. I love asparagus, so I immediately started experimenting with this hybrid vegetable. I like to prepare it in the style of broccoli rabe, with some minor adjustments.

SERVES 2

1 bunch BROCCOLINI	LEMON JUICE to taste
2 tablespoons OLIVE OIL	LEMON ZEST to taste
1–2 minced cloves GARLIC	SEA SALT to taste
1/2 teaspoon CRUSHED RED PEPPER	Grated PECORINO to taste

Bring a large pot of water to a boil.

Blanch the broccolini for 1 minute.

Drain and dunk in a cold bath to stop the cooking process.

Bring a skillet to medium heat, then add the olive oil, garlic, and red pepper.

When the garlic turns golden, add the broccolini and stir to combine (keep an eye on the garlic—it burns easily).

Remove from heat.

Add lemon juice, lemon zest, and sea salt to taste.

Sprinkle broccolini with the grated pecorino.

Sweet AND *Spicy* BUTTERNUT SQUASH

FALL REPRESENTS ALL KINDS OF GREAT THINGS FOR ME: bundling up in my favorite sweats, the crispy morning air when I let my dogs out, the start of holiday parties, and the return of butternut squash. Every year I look forward to seeing the piles of butternut squash, pumpkins, and gourds at the grocery store. I love so many of fall's recipes, but butternut squash provides some of the best. There is no Yankee Candle in the world that could ever come close to duplicating the smell of a butternut squash roasting away, topped with cardamom, nutmeg, and cinnamon. If you have never tried butternut squash, get excited, since you are about to fall in love. Squash can be intimidating, but I promise you can do it—and this step-by-step guide will help. There are two ways to present this recipe, so I will explain as we go.

SERVES 1-2

1 BUTTERNUT SQUASH
EARTH BALANCE or BUTTER, for brushing
OLIVE OIL
1 pinch SEA SALT

1 pinch CAYENNE
1 pinch NUTMEG
1 pinch BROWN SUGAR
Few dollops GOAT CHEESE
1 tablespoon HALF-AND-HALF

Preheat the oven to 375 degrees.

Bring your biggest pot of water to a boil.

Cook butternut squash in hot water for 4–5 minutes (this softens the squash and makes it easier to peel).

Peel the squash and cut it in half lengthwise.

Scoop the seeds out with a spoon.

SLICED

Cut the squash into wedges, like you would a cantaloupe.

Lay the wedges across a baking sheet covered in aluminum foil.

MASHED

Cut the squash into small cubes.

Scatter them across a baking sheet covered in aluminum foil.

Brush Earth Balance or butter across the squash (I like to drizzle a thin layer of olive oil across it too).

Sprinkle with salt, cayenne, and nutmeg.

Bake the squash for 30–40 minutes, checking occasionally.

Cook longer for the mashed version (you want the cubes to fall apart with very little effort from your fork).

IF YOU ARE WATCHING YOUR DIET, BUTTERNUT SQUASH WINS IN THE DEBATE OF BUTTERNUT SQUASH VERSUS SWEET POTATOES TOO. HALF THE CALORIES, CARBS, AND SUGAR! SO THIS THANKSGIVING, OFFER TO MAKE BUTTERNUT SQUASH FOR YOUR FAMILY GATHERING. I PROMISE NO ONE WILL ASK FOR SWEET POTATOES EVER AGAIN.

For sliced version, arrange squash on a serving plate and sprinkle with brown sugar.

For mashed, transfer to a large mixing bowl and mash in the brown sugar and half-and-half.

Serve both versions with a couple dollops of goat cheese.

chapter nine
SUPPER

Simple Grilled Halibut

Mussels and Clams over Linguini

Lemon Caper Chicken

One-Pot Steamed Fish

Grape, Goat Cheese, and Rosemary Pizzette

Legit Prosciutto-Wrapped Chicken with Shallot Sauce

I LEARNED TO MAKE THIS SIMPLE RECIPE IN THE MIDST OF ONE OF MY MOST COMPLICATED RELATIONSHIPS. I had been dating someone for a while, and we were spending a lot of our time together. We were having sleepovers, cooking dinners, and doing all the things cute couples do. Now is the time I should probably mention that it is still unclear to me if we were ever really a couple.

This was my first time experiencing a relationship that was not clear-cut. We would fight, stop seeing each other, make up, and fight again. It was always explosive, but always worth it.

Some of my favorite times with him were spent having family dinner at my mom's house. One night, she made a lemon pepper halibut, and we were immediately hooked. It became our favorite thing to make. My mom actually bought him a grill pan for his house just so that we could make it together, which we did on many occasions. We would drink too much wine and grill our halibut and dance circles around all the things we wanted to say to each other.

2 **HALIBUT** fillets

A drizzle of **OLIVE OIL**

LEMON JUICE, to taste

LEMON ZEST, to taste

A pinch of **SEA SALT**

A pinch of **BLACK PEPPER**

Preheat the oven to 350 degrees.

Bring a nonstick grill pan to medium heat.

Brush fish with olive oil.

Season with lemon juice, lemon zest, salt, and pepper.

Place on pan.

When the fish is halfway done, place the grill pan in the oven for about 4 minutes.

Turn the oven to broil.

Brown the top of the fish for another minute.

Carefully remove the fish from the grill pan and serve.

NOTE: I love this fish served alongside the Herb "Skinny" Salad or the Pecorino and Red Pepper Broccolini.

My friend Yoni suggests you put the lid on and leave it. He claims, "The clams can sense your desperation, so let them do their own thing."

Mussels AND Clams OVER Linguini

THIS RECIPE ORIGINALLY APPEARED ON THE REAL GIRL'S KITCHEN WEBSITE, AND SHORTLY AFTER I POSTED IT, MY FRIEND ERIN BEGAN MAKING IT FOR HER BOYFRIEND ON A REGULAR BASIS. She first cooked it one night when his parents were in town visiting. It was a big hit, and it soon made its way into their weekly dinner rotation.

Erin always sends me pictures of the finished product, and it makes me feel so good to get the support of my friends and family when it comes to my recipes. She makes these mussels and clams so often that, dare I say, her version might be even better than mine.

SERVES 4

16-ounce box FETTUCCINI
1/4 cup OLIVE OIL
1 chopped SHALLOT
3 cloves GARLIC
1 cup DRY WHITE WINE
1 cup VEGETABLE BROTH
1 teaspoon SEA SALT
Sprinkle of CAYENNE PEPPER
1 teaspoon BLACK PEPPER

CRUSHED RED PEPPER to taste
1 teaspoon PAPRIKA
1 whole BAY LEAF (optional)
1 pound MUSSELS
1 pound CLAMS
1 pound peeled and deveined SHRIMP
LEMON WEDGES
1/4 cup chopped FLAT-LEAF PARSLEY

Bring a big pot of water to a boil and add fettuccini.

Cook fettuccini according to package directions, then strain and set aside.

Bring a skillet to medium heat.

Add olive oil and chopped shallot.

Sauté until shallots soften, then add the garlic.

Once the garlic has softened, add the white wine and vegetable broth.

Add salt, cayenne, black pepper, crushed red pepper, paprika, and bay leaf.

Once the broth is nice and bubbly, add mussels, clams, and shrimp.

Boil about 8 minutes, or until the shells have opened.

Add the fettuccini to the pot and toss well.

Squeeze the lemon across the top and add a pinch of sea salt.

Garnish with chopped parsley.

Lemon Caper Chicken

THIS IS ONE OF THE MEALS THAT TRANSPORTS ME BACK TO MY CHILD-HOOD FROM THE MOMENT I TAKE MY FIRST BITE. My mom cooked dinner for us more nights than not, and this was one of my favorites. She stills makes this chicken for us, and we still love every bite.

Now my mom has a huge Meyer lemon tree in her backyard. She will call me and say, "Haylie, I just picked a big basket of lemons off my tree, come over for dinner—I'm making the chicken." Not only do we get to enjoy one of our favorite home-cooked meals, we get to enjoy her homegrown lemons too. Truly the best.

SERVES 2-3

1 teaspoon KOSHER SALT
1 teaspoon BLACK PEPPER
1 teaspoon SEASONING of choice
(I use lemon pepper or another peppery seasoning)
4 tablespoons FLOUR
(gluten-free works)
2–3 CHICKEN CUTLETS

2 LEMONS
2 tablespoons OLIVE OIL
1 cup CHICKEN BROTH
2 tablespoons CAPERS
3 finely minced cloves GARLIC
1 splash HALF-AND-HALF (optional)
PARSLEY to garnish

In a flat dish, combine kosher salt, black pepper, seasoning of choice, and 2 tablespoons of the flour.

Coat the chicken in the mixture.

Zest a bit of the lemon across each cutlet.

Bring a skillet to medium heat, add olive oil, and brown chicken until done, approximately 7 minutes, turning once.

Transfer chicken to a fresh plate.

In a mixing bowl, whisk chicken broth, juice of 1 lemon, capers, and garlic until smooth.

Pour the mixture into the chicken drippings and whisk until combined.

Add a splash of half-and-half if desired.

Add chicken back to pan to warm before serving.

Spoon sauce over each cutlet.

Garnish with capers and parsley.

ONE-POT *Steamed Fish*

I HEAR FROM SO MANY PEOPLE THAT THEY WANT TO INCORPORATE MORE FISH INTO THEIR DIETS BUT ARE INTIMIDATED OR NOT QUITE SURE HOW TO PREPARE IT. This one-pot recipe is a foolproof dish for beginners. While the flavors are very bold and complex, the process is quite simple. There is very little cleanup required, the final product is delicious, and the leftovers can be saved for the next day. Feel free to add some of your favorite vegetables or substitute for any ingredients you don't like.

SERVES 2-4

4–6 peeled and sliced POTATOES
(enough to fit over the bottom
of the pot, creating a bed for the fish)
1 link CHORIZO (if it is large,
use half)
1/2 cup OLIVE OIL
1 chopped and deseeded JALAPEÑO
1 chopped YELLOW ONION
1 red or green BELL PEPPER

3 cloves GARLIC
1 handful CHERRY TOMATOES
32 ounces VEGETABLE BROTH
1 splash TABASCO
1 handful CILANTRO
1 teaspoon KOSHER SALT
1 teaspoon BLACK PEPPER
1 teaspoon LEMON PEPPER
2 HALIBUT FILLETS

Bring a large pot of water to a boil.

Add potatoes and boil until they are almost done.

Remove from heat and set aside.

Discard water.

In a new pot, add the chorizo link and cook on low heat until the casing starts to pop.

Scrape the chorizo out of the casing and discard the casing.

Add olive oil, jalapeño, onion, and bell pepper to the chorizo pot.

Sauté until soft.

Add the garlic and cherry tomatoes and stir, giving them a minute to soften.

Add the vegetable broth, Tabasco, and cilantro, and bring to a boil.

Add the potatoes.

Sprinkle salt, black pepper, and lemon pepper on the fish.

Lay the fish fillets across the bed of potatoes and spoon some of the broth over the fish.

Cover and do not open for 8–10 minutes, depending on the thickness of the fillets.

I'M GOING TO LET YOU IN ON A LITTLE SECRET: I HAVE FOUND ALL KINDS OF WAYS AROUND HAVING TO FACE MY BAKING SHORTCOMINGS HEAD ON. I love making pizzettes, but clearly this real girl isn't making her own dough. If you want to experiment with making your own dough, more power to you. But my favorite way to get homemade-tasting dough is to buy it from any of my favorite pizza places. They will almost always sell it to you, and the finished product benefits from it. I can guarantee you that if I made the dough from scratch, it would be a big hot mess. So have no shame in preparing this pizzette on to-go dough.

SERVES 2

TO-GO DOUGH
OLIVE OIL or WHITE
PIZZETTE SAUCE
½ cup crumbled GOAT CHEESE
10 seedless PURPLE or
GREEN GRAPES

3 stalks ROSEMARY
SEA SALT
CRUSHED RED PEPPER

• •

Preheat the oven to 350 degrees.

Roll out the dough and brush with olive oil or white pizzette sauce (see next page).

Scatter goat cheese across the pizzette.

Add the grapes whole.

Sprinkle rosemary across the top.

Bake for 15–20 minutes, checking every ten minutes.

Finish with a pinch of sea salt and crushed red pepper.

2 tablespoons BUTTER
1 tablespoon FLOUR
1 cup LOW-FAT MILK
2 minced cloves GARLIC

1/4 cup grated PARMIGIANO-REGGIANO
1 pinch KOSHER SALT
1/4 cup grated PECORINO

Bring a small skillet to medium heat.

Melt the butter and whisk in the flour.

Add the milk, garlic, and salt and whisk until smooth.

Add Parmigiano-Reggiano and pecorino.

Stir until melted.

SHALLOT SAUCE:

2 tablespoons OLIVE OIL
1 tablespoon FLOUR
1/2 cup LOW-FAT MILK
2–3 SHALLOTS, sliced
into rings

1/2 cup DRY WHITE WINE
1/2 cup CHICKEN BROTH
BLACK PEPPER

• •

Warm the olive oil on low heat in a skillet.

Whisk flour with milk in a bowl.

Add shallots to the skillet.

Stir for 2–3 minutes or until soft.

Add dry white wine and chicken broth.

Whisk the flour-and-milk mixture into the bubbly broth.

Spoon over chicken when done.

Finish with a grind of fresh black pepper.

I CALL THIS CHICKEN "LEGIT" BECAUSE EVERYONE WHO HAS EVER TRIED IT ALWAYS PROCLAIMS, "THIS CHICKEN IS LEGIT!" AS SOON AS THEY TAKE THEIR FIRST BITE. I have to agree with them. It's to die for.

I first made this chicken for a dinner party at my house. My brother-in-law, Mike, was bringing some of his friends, and my dad was in town, so I had every excuse to show off and flex my culinary muscles. I made roasted bone marrow and a parsley salad as an appetizer, a buttermilk shrimp gazpacho, and this totally legit chicken.

As it turned out, one of Mike's friends was quite the foodie. He spent the majority of the evening in the kitchen with me, asking how I prepare certain dishes and giving me tips on how he makes some of his favorite meals. Each recipe brought up a new topic of discussion, and we had a great evening. I felt so much happiness watching everyone eating and enjoying themselves, and this chicken was definitely the star of the night.

SERVES 4

8-ounce log GOAT CHEESE	BLACK PEPPER
4 CHICKEN BREASTS	1 tablespoon THYME
SEA SALT	20 slices PROSCUITTO

Preheat the oven to 350 degrees.

Bring goat cheese to room temperature.

Slice a pocket down the side of each chicken breast.

Using your fingers, work the pockets open and press goat cheese into the center of each chicken breast.

Season the chicken with salt, black pepper, and thyme leaves.

Wrap the prosciutto around each chicken breast, sealing the pockets.

Lay the chicken in a greased baking dish and bake for 15 minutes or until juices run clear when you slice the chicken.

Serve topped with a spoonful of shallot sauce.

chapter ten
CHEESE
AND
CHARCUTERIE
PLATES

Cheese Boards

Cheese Favorites

Maple Bacon

Rosemary Marcona Almonds

Grilled Asparagus, Mushroom Caps, or Fennel

Parmesan Crisps

Charcuterie

Cheese Boards

A FEW YEARS AGO MY MOM STARTED A CHRISTMAS TRADITION WITH MY BROTHER-IN-LAW'S FAMILY. She makes a very extravagant cheese plate and sends it (along with my sister and brother-in-law) to Newport, to be enjoyed on Christmas Day. It's her way of sending some holiday cheer their way.

I loved her idea so much that I've started doing this with a couple of my friends as well. Every "Real Girl" should know how to throw together a fantastic cheese plate. Cheese is the perfect appetizer for any occasion, and it only takes a tiny bit of knowledge to create a really killer plate. We aren't talking about throwing some grapes and a piece of cheese on a plate with water crackers. We are talking about exciting combinations of sweet and salty, buttery and nutty, and exciting additions that make your plate stand out from the rest.

Here is an easy guide to pairing, but don't feel too attached to any of the combinations. The best plates are the ones full of inspiration and creativity.

A BIG CHEESE PLATE OR BOARD IS THE FIRST STEP.

A rustic wooden plate is always a great look. It feels very "farm to table" and is perfect for a more relaxed setting.

A large piece of slate is my other favorite way to serve cheese. You can use chalk to label your cheeses or decorate your slate (is there anything cuter than sketching out a vintage-looking frame around the plate?).

HOW MANY PEOPLE ARE SNACKING ON THIS PLATE?

I like to work in odd numbers, so I usually choose three to five kinds of cheese. You should plan on about three ounces per person.

ALWAYS ACCESSORIZE.

There is no better time to bust out the cute utensils that (if you are like me) you have collected over the years. As long as you stick to a general theme, the more mismatched, the better. Include a decorative spoon and lots of cheese spreaders or knives. You should have one utensil per cheese to avoid running one flavor into the next.

MAKING A BED FOR THE CHEESE TO LIE IN . . .

When arranging the cheese on a rustic-style plate, I love to add greens because they're a great pop of color. Edible flowers are always a lovely touch too.

Triple-cream brie. Earthy and creamy. Everyone's favorite.

This is a classic cheese plate staple. Everyone loves a creamy brie, and it goes well with just about anything. You really can't go wrong with this guy.

Brie is great with berries, apricots, melon, sun-dried tomatoes, apples, pears, or any juicy fruit, like grapes. The burst of sweetness cuts through the buttery flavor of the brie.

Blue or gorgonzola. Salty and intense. The wild card.

I know a lot of people who don't like blue cheese. I think it's simply because they haven't paired it with the right things. If the blue is too sharp for you, though, try a gorgonzola. It's a bit milder but still packs a great salty punch.

Blue cheese is great with pears, figs, candied pecans, ginger, and bacon.

Maple Bacon:

Preheat the oven to 400 degrees. Bring a skillet to medium heat and cook the bacon until it is almost done, but not crisp. Remove from heat and arrange it on a baking sheet. Brush with maple syrup and place in the oven until bacon is crisp.

ASIAGO OR PARMESAN. SALTY AND NUTTY WITH A GRANULAR TEXTURE. NOT TO BE UNDERESTIMATED.

There are so many cheese blends to choose from that sometimes a cheese plate can get carried away. Asiago is a blend of cheddar and parmesan that is definitely a classic. Asiago and parmesan are also perfect cheeses to pair with charcuterie meats.

Asiago and parmesan go great with marcona almonds, meats, grilled vegetables, and apples.

ROSEMARY MARCONA ALMONDS:

Chop 2 sprigs of rosemary. Toss 1 cup of marcona almonds with rosemary, 1 teaspoon of olive oil, and a pinch of sea salt.

GRILLED ASPARAGUS, MUSHROOM CAPS, OR FENNEL:

Cut vegetables into bite-sized pieces. Place them on a hot grill or grill pan until marks appear. Don't overcook—they should stay crunchy. Drizzle with olive oil or truffle oil and sea salt.

PARMESAN CRISPS:

Preheat the oven to 400 degrees. Line a baking sheet with parchment paper. Grate parmesan into a bowl. Drop cheese onto baking sheet in piles with a 3-inch diameter. Arrange with your fingers into small circles. Bake until melted but not bubbling. Remove from heat and let cool.

DON'T BE AFRAID TO ASK YOUR LOCAL CHEESE SHOP FOR SUGGESTIONS. THEY ARE ALMOST ALWAYS HAPPY TO GIVE YOU A SAMPLE.

A CHARCUTERIE PLATE IS A GREAT KICKOFF TO A DINNER PARTY OR CASUAL GET-TOGETHER. Odd numbers make for a better presentation, so the same rule of three to five items applies. Here are my three favorites.

PROSCIUTTO DI PARMA. MILD AND DELICATE. THE LADY.

I absolutely love prosciutto. I prefer prosciutto di Parma because it has a buttery and nutty flavor, thanks to the whey the cows in France nosh on. It's sweet and delicate and melts in your mouth.

Great with melon, blue cheese, and figs.

BRESAOLA. FRAGRANT AND LEAN. THE GOOD GUY.

Bresaola is incredibly versatile and pairs easily. It can go with just about any of the salty cheeses, and it is wonderful on top of an arugula and parmesan salad. It is fragrant with hints of cloves and cinnamon and has little to no fat.

SALAMI AND SOPRESSATA. HOT AND SALTY. THE BAD BOYS.

Since salami isn't the healthiest of meats, I order mine sliced very thin. I love a peppery salami or hot sopressata, and love them paired with parmesan or asiago.

CHARCUTERIE PLATE ADDITIONS:

Caper berries, miniature pickles, olives, and mustard.

chapter eleven
DESSERTS

Rosemary Olive Oil and Sea Salt over Ice Cream

Crescent Roll Apple Pies

Strawberry Shortcake in a Mason Jar

Nutella Pizza

Chocolate-Covered Bacon and Ice Cream

Oven S'mores

Rosemary Olive Oil AND SEA SALT OVER ICE CREAM

MY MOM SERVED THIS DESSERT AT A DINNER PARTY ONE NIGHT, AND IT WAS A HUGE HIT. The flavors are unexpected and make a great conversation starter. No one could believe that she paired rosemary and vanilla bean ice cream, but everyone went crazy for it. This dish is fresh, vibrant, and not to be missed.

SERVES 4

1 cup OLIVE OIL
1 sprig fresh ROSEMARY
SEA SALT

Good-quality VANILLA BEAN
ICE CREAM

Warm the olive oil and rosemary in a small saucepan over low heat for 20 minutes.

Remove the rosemary.

Transfer the olive oil to a mason jar or bowl.

Let cool.

Drizzle the olive oil over a scoop of ice cream.

Sprinkle with sea salt.

THANK GOD FOR PILLSBURY. *Seriously.* Without them, I would be hopeless when it comes to baking anything, but I love their crescent rolls the most. They're surprisingly versatile, and I can easily turn them into a savory appetizer or a sweet dessert. I even enjoy them plain, and I don't hate on them when they are a day old. So thank you, Pillsbury, for a lot of things. Especially your crescent rolls.

SERVES 2

1 can of PILLSBURY CRESCENT ROLLS

1 sliced RED APPLE

2 tablespoons SPLENDA BROWN SUGAR

• •

Preheat the oven to 350 degrees.

Spray a baking sheet with canola oil.

Lay out the crescent roll triangles on a cutting board.

Roll 1 slice of apple and a pinch of brown sugar into each roll.

Bake according to the directions on the Pillsbury package.

Strawberry
Shortcake

Strawberry Shortcake IN A MASON JAR

I HAVE LOVED READING THE RECIPES FROM MY GREAT-GRAND-MOTHER'S COOKBOOK. I love the smell of the pages when I open the book and how fragile they are. I love the simple approach she took and how easy she made all her recipes look. The only problem is that I can't bake, and this lady was all about desserts.

I have tried and have failed miserably every time. I attempted to make cookies for my neighbors when I first moved into my house, and they came out of the oven like hard little rocks made of something that once resembled cookie dough. Even my box-mix cakes come out dry and oddly shaped. I have learned to accept my dessert shortcomings, and I chalk it up to my lack of ability to follow directions—in the kitchen and in life. Luckily, there are still desserts for people like me—desserts with a lovely presentation that require no measurements and no baking. This strawberry shortcake is a prime example, and it's my absolute favorite way to trick people into thinking I can do it all.

SERVES 4

2 pounds STRAWBERRIES, destemmed, thinly sliced
Juice of 2 LEMONS
2 cups SUGAR

Store-bought ANGEL FOOD CAKE
1 carton HEAVY WHIPPING CREAM
Zest of 1 LIME
4 16-ounce MASON JARS

DAY 1
Mix strawberries, lemon juice, and 1 cup sugar in a bowl.
Let the bowl sit in the refrigerator overnight.

DAY 2
Trace a mason jar with a knife to cut a round piece of angel food cake.
Press the cake into the bottom of the jar.
Layer the strawberries on top.
Add whipped cream.

WHIPPED CREAM:
In a cold metal bowl, slowly mix the cream, a cup of sugar, and lime zest using a hand mixer for about 7 minutes. The mixture will first turn into a bowl of tiny bubbles, then it will slowly turn into a thick, zesty whipped cream.

Nutella Pizza

THIS RECIPE WAS DISCOVERED DURING A TRIP TO DALLAS TO VISIT MY CHILDHOOD BEST FRIEND, CARLY. Her husband took us out for dinner at a great little hole-in-the-wall pizza place, where we had something similar for dessert. We were already so full, but once we saw the table next to us devour one, we made room.

I can't help but get nostalgic when Carly and I are together. We met at Camp Longhorn in fifth grade. Both of us had parents who had gone to Longhorn, and summer camp is a very important part of a Texas childhood.

At Camp Longhorn, kids from all over the country bus in to spend three weeks in the middle of the Texas hill country. The camp has floating cabins and a big water pillow called "the blob." There are skit-filled campfires every night, group swims, camp carnivals, dance nights, and, of course, boys. I loved everything about Longhorn. On my second-year arrival day, as I was making up my bed and meeting all the girls in my cabin, a tiny blond firecracker came storming in the front door. Carly was rapping every word to a 2Pac song as she chose the bed next to mine. Then, in a fantastic Texas accent, she said, "Hi, I'm Carly from Tyler, Texas."

We made friends that very first day, and seventeen years later she is still one of my best friends. Our Camp Longhorn adventures were the kinds of things other campers wrote home about. I wish I could list all the mischief that Carly and I got into at Longhorn, but we never got caught for most of it, so I probably shouldn't rat us out now. After all, we are going to want to send our kids there someday. Suffice it to say that we dominated during the nightly cabin raids, and we each married at least three boys "in holy macaroni" at every camp carnival.

Camp wouldn't have been the same without Carly, and neither would my life. But as great as our childhood memories are, we have even better memories as adults. I'll never forget how special it was to see Carly's face in the audience as I starred in my first Broadway show or how proud I was to hang one of her paintings in my home. I'll never forget doing her makeup for her wedding. I'll never forget how beautiful she looked as she beamed "I do" to her husband, Blake, or how loved I felt when she flew to LA to be with me after my big breakup. I love that when we see each other, it's like no time has passed. I love that we still love each other as much as we did that first summer at Camp Longhorn.

1 TORTILLA
NUTELLA
1 sliced BANANA
POWDERED SUGAR to garnish
1 tablespoon crushed WALNUTS

Warm tortilla in a skillet over medium heat
until both sides are crispy.
Spread Nutella across the warm tortilla.
Arrange banana slices on the tortilla.
Sprinkle with powdered sugar and walnuts.
Slice like pizza.

Chocolate-Covered Bacon AND ICE CREAM

IT PROBABLY GOES WITHOUT SAYING THAT THIS IS ONE NAUGHTY DESSERT. It combines three ultimate cheat treats and I couldn't be happier about that. I first made this dish for my sister when she was pregnant. Then I made it for a girlfriend who was going through a rough breakup, and now I make it for my sweet-toothed boyfriend. It is a super simple dessert that can be made in fifteen minutes or less.

SERVES 4

1 package BACON
12-ounce bag CHOCOLATE CHIPS

VANILLA BEAN ICE CREAM

Heat skillet to medium-high heat.

Add bacon to skillet and cook until crisp.

Remove from skillet and press slices between paper towels.

Let cool completely.

In a small sauce pan, warm the chocolate until melted, stirring to prevent burning.

Using a pastry brush, paint chocolate down the sides of each strip of bacon.

Place bacon in refrigerator for a few minutes, until the chocolate is hardened.

Arrange over a bowl of ice cream.

NOTE: The trickiest part of this dessert is not eating the bacon before it makes it to the ice cream bowl. Hope you have better luck than I do.

Oven S'mores

I DISCOVERED THE OVEN S'MORE TECHNIQUE WHEN MY BOYFRIEND WANTED TO MAKE THEM ONE NIGHT. It was such a cute and romantic idea. We didn't have a fire pit and decided to try out the oven. Instead of setting the oven to 350 degrees, we sparked the broiler. He thought it would make the edges crispy, the way a real fire would, and the heat would still melt the chocolate. I think there is nothing cuter than watching a guy problem-solve in the kitchen.

We built a pan of s'mores, sprinkled some cinnamon across the top, and put them in a hot oven. They came out perfect, and if you are wondering how long they should stay in there . . . kiss for a minute and a half. They should be ready.

SERVES 2

| HONEY GRAHAM CRACKERS | MARSHMALLOWS |
| CHOCOLATE BAR | CINNAMON |

Turn on the broiler and let the oven get really hot.

Break the graham crackers in half.

Place a piece of chocolate on each graham cracker.

Top each with a marshmallow.

Sprinkle with cinnamon.

Place the tray of s'mores under the broiler.

Watch closely—they will burn quickly if you aren't careful!

chapter twelve

ESK
(EVERYBODY SHOULD KNOW)

Roasted Garlic

Simple Grilled Chicken Breast

Sun-Dried Tomatoes

Roasted Red Peppers

Guacamole

Roasted Garlic

I LOVE ROASTED GARLIC BECAUSE YOU CAN USE IT FOR SO MANY DIFFERENT DISHES, AND IT ALWAYS ADDS A GREAT DYNAMIC PUNCH OF FLAVOR. It's delicious in all kinds of soups or spread across a warm piece of bread.

Preheat the oven to 350 degrees.

Slice the top off of each head of garlic.

Drizzle with olive oil, a pinch of salt, and a sprig of rosemary (optional).

Wrap each head in aluminum foil and bake for 20 minutes.

Slide each clove of garlic out of its skin with a knife.

IT PROBABLY GOES WITHOUT SAYING THAT THIS IS A NO-BRAINER ESK. Grilled chicken breast is the ultimate salad topper, a great way to eat healthy and get a quick protein fix.

Bring a skillet or grill pan to medium heat.

Add a drop of olive oil to the warm pan.

Season chicken breast with salt and pepper.

Cook chicken for 6 minutes on each side, until juices run clear when the chicken is poked with a fork.

SUN-DRIED TOMATOES ARE A GREAT STAPLE TO KEEP IN YOUR HOUSE, AND HOMEMADE ONES ARE EVEN BETTER. Add to salads, cheese plates, or dips like hummus. There are many ways to go about making these. The real deal sun-dried tomatoes cook in the sunshine for about a week (cover with a cheesecloth during the day and bring them in overnight). The oven variety cook in a low-heat oven for about eight hours. However you choose to go about making them, the result is always the same. A sweet and zesty, perfect sun-dried tomato.

Preheat the oven to 250 degrees.

Slice the tomatoes lengthwise.

Remove the seeds and excess juice.

Season with sea salt and oregano.

Arrange on a baking sheet and bake for about 8 hours.

ROASTED *Red Peppers*

PERFECT FOR LAYERING ON A GREAT SANDWICH, paired with salted ricotta cheese, or chopped into a salad . . . ESK how to roast a red pepper.

Turn on your stove burner.

Lay peppers directly on the grates.

Use tongs to turn the peppers so they get evenly charred (they will hiss and crackle a bit—don't be alarmed).

Once evenly charred, immediately place peppers in a large bowl and cover with a plate or aluminum foil.

Let steam for about 5 minutes.

Peel the skins off.

Slice open the peppers and remove the stems and seeds.

Guacamole

EVERY TIME I EAT GUACAMOLE, IT REMINDS ME OF A LATE NIGHT WITH TWO OF MY SOUL MATES. We met on the set of a movie about a college pact in which, if the main character and her best guy friend don't marry anyone in ten years, then they will marry each other. Well, years later the college boyfriend tracks her down only to find that she is getting married to someone else in ten days. I fell madly in (friend) love with the two men who played my college boyfriend and my current fiancé. The three of us quickly became inseparable.

One night after filming, we got together to have a couple of beers at one of their houses and relax after a long work week. We sat on the porch, watched the sun go down, and talked about life. They both have such different perspectives on things, which at times led to some fiery debates. I was all too happy to be front row, watching it go down. A couple of beers turned into quite a few beers and a couple of bottles of wine. Pretty soon we were raiding the fridge for something to snack on. The only items in my friend's house were crackers, avocados, goat cheese, some onions, garlic left over from a food-delivery service, and some salt and pepper that came in mini airplane-shaped shakers because . . . well . . . he had taken them from an airplane. Due to my drunken hunger, I quickly tossed together all the ingredients and tried to convince them I was making us guacamole. If I remember correctly, the airplane saltshaker was empty, so we used a leftover soy sauce packet for seasoning. This was the most awful guacamole ever, but we had so much fun. At sunrise we finally went to sleep like a bunch of drunk puppies in a pile. There is actually photographic evidence of our drunken shenanigans, but we have sworn that it will remain in our friendship vault.

SERVES 2

2 AVOCADOS	1 chopped and deseeded TOMATO
Juice of 1 LIME	1 generous pinch SEA SALT
1 chopped and deseeded JALAPEÑO	1 generous pinch BLACK PEPPER
1 handful chopped CILANTRO	1 pinch CAYENNE

Mash all the ingredients in a serving bowl.

NOTE: To make creamy guacamole, add 1 tablespoon of Greek yogurt.

Homemade dressings are a great way to avoid processed dressings that are filled with hidden fat and preservatives. Here are a couple of my favorites.

chapter thirteen
DRESSINGS

Real Girl's Kitchen Basic Vinaigrette

Zesty Ranch Dressing

Lemon Tahini Dressing

MAKING HOMEMADE SALAD DRESSINGS ALWAYS REMINDS ME OF MY MOTHER. When I was a kid, our refrigerator was constantly filled with those old-school premeasured salad dressing containers. My sister and I would argue over who got to fill them, and based on good behavior my mom would give one of us the honors.

This basic vinaigrette is a no brainer. It pairs well with any greens, and you will more than likely already have all these ingredients in your kitchen. If not, don't be scared to substitute different types of vinegars. You can store this vinaigrette in a jar in your refrigerator for a couple of weeks.

SERVES 4

1/3 cup OLIVE OIL
1 tablespoon finely chopped SHALLOT
1/3 cup CHAMPAGNE VINEGAR
1 teaspoon DIJON MUSTARD

1 teaspoon WHOLE-GRAIN MUSTARD
1 tablespoon AGAVE or HONEY
1 pinch SEA SALT and BLACK PEPPER

Start with the olive oil and whisk in remaining ingredients until blended.

Zesty Ranch DRESSING

GROWING UP, I PUT RANCH ON EVERYTHING: VEGGIES, SALAD, AND OF COURSE PIZZA. My friend Hannah loves ranch dressing. I always keep ranch dressing and fresh vegetables in my refrigerator so I have a snack for her. We love this chunky version because it is a healthy take on a childhood favorite.

SERVES 8

1 small handful fresh THYME
1 small handful fresh OREGANO
1 small handful fresh MARJORAM
7 chopped stalks CELERY
3 peeled and chopped CARROTS
1 chopped bunch GREEN ONIONS
1 deseeded JALAPEÑO
3 cloves GARLIC

Juice of 1 LEMON
16 ounces LOW-FAT COTTAGE CHEESE
16 ounces FAT-FREE GREEK YOGURT
1 teaspoon KOSHER SALT
Lots of BLACK PEPPER

Blend all ingredients in a food processor or high-powered blender.

ONE OF MY FAVORITE WAYS TO ENJOY THIS RANCH IS ON BAKED CHICKEN. BRUSH IT ACROSS BOTH SIDES OF A CHICKEN BREAST, DREDGE EACH BREAST IN PANKO BREADCRUMBS, AND BAKE AT 375 FOR 20 MINUTES OR UNTIL DONE.

Lemon Tahini DRESSING

IF YOU HAVE NEVER HEARD OF NUTRITIONAL YEAST, DON'T BE ASHAMED. Neither had I until it was a key ingredient in a recipe I was trying. It is now one of my favorite ingredients! It sort of resembles fish food, but don't be scared. It adds a great cheesiness to any salad, especially kale. You can find it at Whole Foods, specialty markets, or online.

SERVES 6

1/4 cup TAHINI
1/4 cup NUTRITIONAL YEAST
3 cloves GARLIC
1/2 cup fresh LEMON JUICE (juice of about 2 lemons)
4 tablespoons OLIVE OIL

1 teaspoon SEA SALT
1 teaspoon BLACK PEPPER
1/2 teaspoon PAPRIKA (optional)
3 tablespoons or more WATER (adjust to desired consistency)

Combine all ingredients in a small bowl and whisk vigorously to combine.

chapter fourteen
TIPS
AND TOOLS

Frozen Grapes

Peeling Garlic in a Mason Jar

Olive Oil Hand Moisturizer

Mandolin

Salad Spinner

The Boiling Point

Floss or String for Cutting Cheese

Rose Petals for Decorating Cupcakes

EVERY TIME MY GRANDMOTHER COOKED AT OUR HOUSE, I CAN REMEMBER HER SAYING, "IT WOULD TASTE BETTER, BUT I DON'T HAVE ALL MY POTS." I never really understood what she was talking about, mainly because I loved her cooking and couldn't imagine it being better than what it already was. But now that I have my own pots and pans, I get it. Nothing feels as good as cooking in your own kitchen. You know exactly how certain skillets heat and the hot spots in your oven. When it's time to start chopping, you know the sharpest knife in the caddy. I have to admit, I'm particular about using MY kitchenware, but I travel so much that I have learned to make do with whatever is around.

I found some of my favorite kitchen tricks simply through trial and error, and luckily most of my favorite tools are easy to pack. I have been known to fill my salad spinner with underwear and my Vitamix with socks and pack them in my carryon luggage. This practice has gotten me some strange looks going through security, but I make no apologies. I can almost always convince them that a garlic press is not a threat to anything except a clove of garlic.

Here are some of my favorite tools and tips in the kitchen . . . and blank pages for you to add yours as well.

Tips AND *Tools*

FROZEN GRAPES

Frozen grapes are handy for all types of things. I love to peel and freeze big green grapes before I have dinner parties. They act as ice cubes and keep your white wine crisp and cool.

PEELING GARLIC IN A MASON JAR

Don't waste time trying to peel garlic by hand. Place it in a jar, and a couple of shakes is all you need.

OLIVE OIL HAND MOISTURIZER

Anytime I make massaged-kale salads, I love to rub any excess olive oil into my skin before rinsing my hands. Cooking can give your hands a beating, and olive oil is a great way to remoisturize without missing a beat.

MANDOLIN

I use this bad boy on a regular basis. It's the easiest way to slice the veggies for the Herb "Skinny" Salad, and I love the easy cleanup. Plus, the precision slicing always gives your dishes a "professional chef" quality. Love that.

SALAD SPINNER

For some reason, a salad spinner seems like such a throwback for me. Maybe it's because when I was a kid we didn't have pre-bagged salad like we do now. My job was always to clean the greens before our meals. I love how a salad spinner gets the leaves nice and dry without flattening them. It worked like a dream then, and it works like a dream now.

THE BOILING POINT

I can't take full credit for this trick. I actually learned about it from some random e-mail forward my mom sent a couple of years ago, but it has earned an important spot in my kitchen-trick arsenal. It's simple. Place a wooden spoon over the top of a pot; the handle will stop the water from boiling over.

FLOSS OR STRING FOR CUTTING CHEESE

My favorite way to slice soft cheese is with a simple string or floss. Wrap the floss around two of your fingers and press right through.

Tips AND Tools

ROSE PETALS FOR DECORATING CUPCAKES

As you know, I don't bake my own cupcakes. I do, however, love to decorate them! My favorite rose petal trick is perfect for catching any wax that might roll down birthday candles as you make your wish. So take your time and make your wish a good one.

Notes

Notes

chapter fifteen
HERBS

Flat-Leaf Parsley

Sage

Dill

Basil

Cilantro

Rosemary

Herbs de Provence

Mint

Thyme

I'M A HUGE ADVOCATE OF USING FRESH HERBS AS OFTEN AS POSSIBLE. Some recipes require the dried variety, but if you can go the fresh route, you should. Fresh herbs are always available in the grocery store, and most of them are very easy to grow in a window pot or in your backyard.

Flat-Leaf Parsley

Flat-leaf parsley gets most of the attention in my kitchen. I garnish dishes like white wine mussels with it or scatter it across the top of a great piece of chicken. Flat-leaf parsley is really fantastic as a standout flavor too. I love to toss flat-leaf parsley, radishes, lemon juice, olive oil, and sea salt in a bowl and snack away.

Sage

Sage is great placed inside a roasted chicken or scattered across fresh scrambled eggs, but I love sage on all kinds of vegetables. Warm butter with fresh sage and toss butternut squash, turnips, carrots, parsnips, or beets into it. Still looking for something else to do with sage? Wrap a bundle of it with string and burn throughout your house to ward off evil spirits.

DILL

I use dill to make all kinds of dips. My favorite combination is Greek yogurt, garlic, parmesan cheese, lemon, sea salt, and dill. Like flat-leaf parsley, it's a great standout on its own. Chop it into a salad, or bake carrots with olive oil, pepper, sea salt, and chopped dill.

BASIL

I feel like this is the herb that people are most familiar with. The obvious choices for this herb are things like caprese salad or marinara sauce. Sure, those are great way to enjoy basil, but its possibilities are endless. Try tossing strawberries, spinach, feta, balsamic vinegar, and basil together for a refreshing salad.

CILANTRO

Cilantro is the herb that gets the strongest reaction from people. They either love it or hate it, and there are quite a few studies out there that claim some people might actually have a genetic predisposition against it. To some people it tastes like soapsuds. To others it's a vibrant addition to all kinds of soups and guacamole.

ROSEMARY

Rosemary is another one of my favorite herbs. It can be used in everything! It's great with fruit (like oranges), fish, chicken, and lamb. My favorite thing to do with rosemary is to infuse it into olive oil and vinegars. It's also great sprinkled across bread, like focaccia, or roasted potatoes. Herbs de Provence wouldn't be the same without it.

HERBS DE PROVENCE

2 tablespoons dried rosemary
2 tablespoons dried sage
2 tablespoons dried savory
2 tablespoons dried basil
2 tablespoons dried marjoram
2 tablespoons dried thyme
1 teaspoon fennel seeds
1 teaspoon dried lavender

MINT

Mint comes in all kinds of varieties. I grow spearmint, peppermint, and pineapple mint in my backyard. It grows fast, and luckily there are all kinds of ways to use it. Mint is great in salads or as a part of a dipping sauce that pairs with lamb. It's a staple in many popular cocktails, but I love it steeped in hot water. Hot mint tea aids in digestion, calms nerves, helps to cure headaches, relieves stress, and freshens your breath. Bring water to a boil and fill the teapot with mint leaves. Let steep for 5 minutes.

THYME

Thyme is a pungent, spicy herb. It's great paired with rosemary, and a little goes a long way. It's wonderful with meat, fish, and vegetables, and I love it paired with mushrooms.

chapter sixteen
DOG TREATS

BENTLEY'S BLEND

BAKED DOG TREATS

I ADOPTED BENTLEY WHEN I WAS SEVENTEEN YEARS OLD, AND HE BECAME MY BEST FRIEND FOR TEN YEARS. Bentley quickly learned how to be a world traveler. He lived with me in different cities for months at a time, and on any given day you could find him hanging out on the front steps of my trailer door on set. Everywhere I went, Bentley came along too.

One of my favorite Bentley memories happened during an appearance on *Live with Regis and Kelly*. He snuck out of my dressing room and somehow followed my voice until he found me. Everyone was shocked to see this little white dog running out onto the stage, but in typical Bentley fashion, he got his way and spent the rest of the segment on my lap.

We all used to joke that Bentley was "on his last dog life, destined to come back as a human," but I really believe it. We had our own body language, and he required very little use of common dog commands. I loved him so much, and I was always proud when people raved about how much they loved him too.

As Bentley got older, his knees began to give out. Although I had to carry him most places, losing his mobility didn't slow him down. It did, however, affect his appetite.

I read that homemade dog food had the ability to help sick dogs and improve their appetites. Willing to do anything to postpone the inevitable, I started making this blend for him and saw a difference in his attitude immediately. He was excited to eat at every meal and even started to put a little weight back on. Eventually, I had to say goodbye to my little guy. I still miss him like crazy.

NOTE: FOR SOMETHING SPECIAL, YOU CAN ADD CHICKEN LIVERS. THEY ARE INEXPENSIVE TO PURCHASE AT THE GROCERY STORE, AND YOUR PUP WILL BE OVER THE MOON.

1–2 cups no-sodium BROWN RICE

1 pound CHICKEN BREAST

1-pound bag no-sodium FROZEN PEAS

1-pound bag no-sodium FROZEN CARROTS

1 tablespoon FLAX SEEDS

1 tablespoon OMEGA OIL FOR DOGS

Cook the brown rice (don't add salt!).

Boil the chicken and set aside to cool.

Drop peas and carrots into the hot water and remove from heat once they are no longer frozen.

Chop chicken into small cubes.

Toss in veggies, flax seeds, and omega oil.

Serve and watch your dog lick his chops.

BAKED *Dog Treats*

MY LITTLE DOG CHICKEN LOVES THESE BAKED DOG TREATS. I adopted her a year ago, and I love to spoil her rotten. If you giggled at her name, let me explain.

I had just ended a long relationship and vowed to stay single for a year, no matter who came along. Of course, the universe decided to set a great guy right in my lap. I met him around the same time I adopted Chicken. When he met her, he suggested naming her Chicken Burrito, because she did in fact look like a chicken burrito. I thought, "No way am I letting *some guy* name my dog. If we don't work out I'll be reminded of him every day." I really liked him but decided it was best for me to stick to my original single gal plan. Shortly after, the guy and I cordially went separate ways. I named her Kenzie and that was that.

Well, the universe has a funny sense of humor because a year later I'm in the happiest relationship with the previously mentioned guy. I no longer refer to him as *some guy*, instead opting for *my guy* . . . and as for Kenzie, she has gone back to her original name too. Chicken.

YIELD: 25 TREATS

2 ½ cups **WHOLE WHEAT FLOUR**
2 **EGGS**
½ cup **CANNED PUMPKIN**

2 tablespoons **PEANUT BUTTER**
½ teaspoon **GROUND CINNAMON**
1 tablespoon **FLAX SEEDS**

Preheat oven to 350 degrees.

Stir together the flour, eggs, pumpkin, peanut butter, cinnamon, and flax seeds in a bowl.

Add water as needed to help make the dough workable. (The dough should be dry and firm.)

Roll the dough into a 1/2-inch-thick slab. Cut into 1/2-inch pieces.

Bake in preheated oven until hard, about 40 minutes.

Acknowledgments

The biggest thank you's go to Suzanne Lyon and Britton Schey. They found my little blog and plucked it right out of obscurity. I will never forget cooking with you two in the tiny office kitchen at WME while we prepped for the sales meetings for this book, or how Suzanne and I literally ran across town to bring the first hard copy of it to Britton's new office. I am so thankful to call you both friends and will be forever grateful to both of you for believing in me and my food.

Next, my whole team at Razorbill/Penguin. Caroline Donofrio and Ben Schrank, I knew I wanted to make this book with you two the minute we sat down together. I have felt inspired and encouraged to make a book that I am truly passionate about from day one and I have both of you to thank for that. Thank you for trusting in me enough to give me that freedom.

Thank you to the entire sales, marketing, and publicity team. Thank you to Felicia Frazier, who taught me what a true sparkle moment feels like.

Oh, and an apology to Don Weisberg and Ben Schrank, who had to be the only two men in a meeting of a bunch of rowdy women. One of the most fun meetings, thank you!

Kristin Smith and Greg Stadnyk, I can't begin to express how grateful I am to have had you both when it came time to hand over all my work and place it in the hands of a design team. We all had the same vision from day one and you made the book even more beautiful than I could have ever imagined.

Thank you to Vivian Kirklin, Elizabeth Tingue, and Becca Kilman for catching my mistakes and keeping us all on track.

Thank you to my managers, Susan and Cameron Curtis, for being the first people to ever take a chance on me and for being so understanding when I told you that I would be (basically) taking a year off from acting to write a cookbook. I love you both.

Thank you to Jad Dayeh, Margaret Riley, and the rest of my team at William Morris Endeavor.

A big thank you to Kathy Delgado and VintageWeave. Who so lovingly opened up her beautiful store to me. Her vintage French finds gave character and history to every photograph.

Thank you to Sophia Rossi and HelloGiggles for being the first place to ever post a Real Girl's Kitchen recipe.

Hannah Skvarla and Yoni Goldberg. What a team. Hannah, without your organization, secret Pinterest boards, shot lists, and large iced coffees, I would have never finished this book. Truly, the glue. You are the most giving, loyal, and wonderful friend. You keep me inspired. I learn from you every day. I look forward to many many adventures with you. Yoni, that first day of shooting in Ojai seems like years ago. The fashion and model photographer transformed into the food photographer overnight. To work with you on this has been such a gift. You have the ability to capture exactly what I see in my head and in my heart. To many more, friend.

Thank you to my wonderful friends who gave their time or appeared in this book. Xander Ritz, Max Ritz, Ashley Cordova, Erin Haggerty, Carly Allen-Martin, Tyler Hoechlin, Brittany Dier, Beverley Mitchell-Cameron, Drew Rendell, Kristin Murphy, and Maggie Guerin. This experience wouldn't have been the same without your energy and neither would my life.

Thank you to the little cottage by the beach that changed my life in so many ways. To all the inspiration that surrounded me in Venice and to the big kitchen window, where I sat and wrote every single word of this book.

Finally, my family. My wonderful, supportive, amazing family. You have no idea how fun (and difficult!) it was to sort through so many memories. Most of all my sister, Hilary, for being the ultimate partner in crime. I love you, sis. Thick as thieves till the end. ✗